Books Available By Dan Clark:

The Art of Significance: Achieving the Level Beyond Success

Chicken Soup for the College Soul

The Most Popular Stories by Dan Clark in Chicken Soup for the Soul

Puppies for Sale (children's illustrated hardcover)

The Funniest Things Happen When You Look for Laughs

The Priviledge of the Platform: The Art and Science of Public Speaking

The Thrill of Teaching

Wisdom, Rhymes, and Wizardry

Lyrical Poetry

Order at his website: www.danclarkspeak.com

So Have I

Have you ever been alone in a crowded room that's full of lies
Have you ever been betrayed and don't know why
Have you ever felt the backbite of a friend they then deny
You are not alone, so have I—You are not alone, so have I

Have you ever been lonely in a lovers arms and cry
Have you ever hurt from a brutal bad good bye
Have you ever sobbed so long you drained your feelings drip-dry
You are not alone, so have I—You are not alone, so have I

Yea I've felt your pain, it's rained, it's poured on my parade
Yea I've suffered through your blues of knowing I've been played
So when you hear this too shall pass away, tomorrow's just a day away,
and you hang on for one more day, and say . . . I'll try . . . So have I

Have you ever been afraid that no one needs you in their life
Have you ever thought that love has passed you by
Have you ever stopped believing in yourself and died inside
You are not alone, so have I—You are not alone, so have I

I have faced my fears and demons
I have beat the odds
I have realized I can only count on me and God
I have been a broken winged bird but now I fly
I pray, you'll say, so have I

Yea I've felt your pain, it's rained, it's poured on my parade
Yea I've suffered through your blues of knowing I've been played
So when you hear this too shall pass away, tomorrow's just a day away,
and you hang on for one more day, and say . . . I'll try . . . So have I . . . So have I.

Soul Food

Stories
to Keep You Mentally Strong, Emotionally Awake & Ethically Straight

Dan Clark

New York Times Bestselling Author
& Hall of Fame Speaker

Health Communications, Inc.
Deerfield Beach, Florida

www.hcibooks.com

**The Library of Congress Cataloging-in-Publication Data
is available through the Library of Congress**

ISBN-13: 978-0-7573-1725-5 (trade paper)
ISBN-10: 0-7573-1725-1 (trade paper)
ISBN-13: 978-0-7573-1726-2 (e-book)
ISBN-10: 0-7573-1726-X (e-book)

Publisher: Health Communications, Inc.
       3201 S.W. 15th Street
       Deerfield Beach, FL 33442–8190

Cover design by Dane Wesolko
Interior design and formatting by Lawna Patterson Oldfield

Contents

Understanding

Self-Worth

Inspirational

Perspective

Significance

Attitude

Communication

Life Lessons

Commitment

Legacy

Military

Lyrical Poetry

Acknowledgments

To my mother Ruby, who instilled in me a love for reading, writing, and telling stories; and to my beloved Kelly, Danny, Nikola, McCall, and Alexandrea, who have always supported me to do so.

Introduction

We must be willing to pay any price and travel any distance to associate with extraordinary people. Until we do, we should read about these people, learn from them, and be inspired by their stories.

Stories are our greatest teachers because our greatest teachers always tell stories. Educators who think they must follow and complete a scheduled outline regardless of the outcome may be presenting the curriculum, but they may not be teaching. Teaching means the student "gets it." True teachers teach people, not subject matter. The greatest teachers in history taught with parables and stories.

The power of a story is immeasurable. Because life is a story and everybody has one, we connect most quickly and deeply, and communicate most clearly, with stories. When we watch the news, we don't remember the facts and figures. We remember the interpretation of the information. We want to know the relevant meaning and how it specifically relates to our individual circumstances. Facts are retained by the cognitive left brain. Stories are retained by the emotional right brain. The difference is similar to hearing versus listening, understanding versus being understood, being fed versus being nourished.

For example, there was a huge snowstorm one winter in Utah. It forced the huge deer population down from their natural mountain habitat into the villages where they could find food. Because the deer were suddenly caught in public parks and stranded by fences in developed areas, the wildlife management agencies brought in truckloads of hay and spread it around for the deer. The starving deer ate the hay, but hundreds of them still died! Why? When the authorities conducted autopsies, they found the deer's stomachs full of hay. The deer had been fed, but they had not been nourished.

Stories nourish our souls. Stories are mental meals. I write my stories so that when readers don't know what to say, they still have something to share. When a friend or loved one loses someone, goes through a devastating divorce, or is let go from their job, do you feel compelled to say something but don't know what to say? Give this book to them with a note telling them to read a certain story. Let the story speak for you and convey the proper emotionally healing concern, love, and counsel that you want to communicate.

People often ask me if all my stories are true. The answer is yes, absolutely, because my stories always teach true and correct principles crafted in a way so anyone who reads them is inspired to better govern themselves. For this reason, *Soul Food* never becomes obsolete, out of date, or stored on a shelf as old, previously read material. One story might mean more to you a month after you first read it. That is also why *Soul Food* is part of my desktop resource library. Enjoy, reread, share, and keep in touch at www.danclarkspeak.com.

Understanding

Puppies for Sale

A store owner was tacking a sign above his door that read "Puppies for Sale." Signs like that have a way of attracting small children, and, sure enough, a little boy appeared under the store owner's sign.

"How much are you going to sell the puppies for?" he asked.

The store owner replied, "Anywhere from thirty to fifty dollars."

The little boy reached into his pocket and pulled out some change. "I have two dollars and thirty-seven cents," he said. "Can I please look at them?"

The store owner smiled and whistled, and out of the kennel came Lady, who ran down the aisle of his store followed by five tiny balls of fur. One puppy was lagging considerably behind. Immediately, the little boy singled out the lagging, limping puppy and said, "What's wrong with that little dog?"

The store owner explained that the veterinarian had examined the little puppy and had discovered it didn't have a hip socket. It would always limp. It would always be lame. The little boy became excited. "That is the little puppy that I want to buy."

The store owner said, "No, you don't want to buy that little dog. If you really want him, I'll just give him to you."

The little boy got upset. He looked straight into the store owner's eyes, pointed his finger, and said, "I don't want you to just give him to me. That little dog is worth every bit as much as all the other dogs and I'll pay full price. In fact, I'll give you two dollars and thirty-seven cents now and fifty cents a month until I have him paid for."

The store owner countered, "You really don't want to buy this little dog. He is never going to be able to run and jump and play with you like the other puppies."

To this, the little boy reached down and rolled up his pant leg to reveal a badly twisted, crippled left leg supported by a big metal brace. He looked up at the store owner and softly replied, "Well, I don't run so well myself, and this little puppy will need someone who understands."

Puppy Love

The young boy who had been wearing a steel brace on his left leg for the last four months walked through the front door of his home with a newly purchased puppy in his arms. The dog didn't have a hip socket, and it walked with a serious limp. The boy's selection of a physically challenged puppy intrigued his parents. The boy had been down-and-out, but with his new companion at his side, they sensed a newly revitalized spirit of hope and enthusiasm emerging from his soul.

The next day the young boy and his mom went to see a veterinarian to find out how he could best help his little dog. The doctor explained that if he stretched and massaged his puppy's leg every morning and then walked with him at least one mile per day, the muscles around his missing hip would eventually strengthen, and the puppy would have no pain and less of a limp.

Although the dog whimpered and barked out his discomfort, and the boy winced and hassled with his own leg brace, for the next two months, they religiously kept to their massage and walking rehabilitation regimen. By the third month, they were walking three miles every morning before school, and they were both walking without pain.

One Saturday morning as they returned from their workout, a cat leaped out of the bushes and startled the dog. Ripping the leash from the boy's grip, the dog darted into oncoming traffic. With a speeding truck only seconds away, the boy instinctively ran into the street, dove for his dog, and rolled into the gutter. He was too late. The dog was hit and was bleeding profusely from the mouth. As the boy lay there crying and hugging his dying dog, he noticed that his own leg brace had bent and popped loose. With no time to worry about himself, he sprang to his feet, picked up his dog, cuddled it close to him, and started for home. The dog quietly barked, giving him hope and turning the boy's jog into an all-out sprint.

His mother rushed him and his suffering pup to the pet hospital. As they anxiously waited to see if his dog would survive the surgery, he asked his mother why he could now walk and run.

"You had osteomyelitis, which is a disease of the bone," she said. "It weakened and crippled your leg, which caused you to limp in severe pain. Your brace was for support. It wasn't necessarily a permanent condition if you were willing to fight through the pain and hours of therapy. You responded well to the medication, but you always resisted our encouragement for physical therapy, and your father and I didn't know what to do. The doctors told us you were about to lose your leg. But then you brought home your special puppy. It was amazing how you looked at each other day after day and seemed to understand each other's needs. Ironically, as you were helping him, you were actually helping yourself to strengthen and grow. You obviously no longer need the support of a brace, and today you discovered it."

Just then the operating room door slowly opened. Out walked the veterinarian with a smile on his face. "Your dog is going to make it," he said.

The boy learned that when you lose yourself, you find yourself. It is more blessed to give than to receive.

Always Look on the Bright Side

A father promised his son that if he practiced, all day he'd play baseball with him after work. The father arrived home, and they went into the backyard.

"Show me what you can do," the father said. The little boy shuffled his feet, threw the ball up in the air, took a swing, and missed. "Strike one," said the dad.

The son repositioned his feet, threw the ball up again, took a second swing, and missed again. His father said, "Strike two."

More determined than ever, the kid dug in deeper, threw the ball higher, and took a third mighty swing. He missed again, spun completely around, and fell on the ground. His father said, "Strike three, you're out. What do you think about that?"

The youngster stood up, brushed himself off, and said, "Man, am I a good pitcher!"

Broken Doll

A young girl was leaving for school, and her mother reminded her to come straight home when her last class ended. Thirty minutes late, she finally walked through the front door. Her mother scolded her. "Where have you been?" she asked. "I've been worried sick."

With a concerned face the daughter sweetly replied, "I walked home with my friend, Sally, and she dropped her doll and it broke all to pieces. It was just awful!"

Her mother inquired, "So you were late because you stayed to help her pick up the pieces of the doll and put it back together again?"

"Oh no, Mommy," she explained. "I didn't know how to fix the doll. I just stayed to help her cry!"

What Goes Around Comes Around

A unique directive was initiated at a high school in northern Utah, where students with a physical or mental challenge were fully integrated into the mainstream classes and curriculum. To make it work, the administration organized a mentor program that teamed up one special-needs student with a mainstream student who would help him or her along.

The athletic director presented the idea to the captain of the football team. John was a tall, strong, intense young man—not the patient, caring type needed for this kind of program. He made it clear that this "wasn't his thing" and he didn't have time to be a mentor. But the athletic director knew it would be good for him and insisted that John volunteer.

John was matched up with Randy—a young man with Down syndrome. Reluctant and irritated at first, John literally tried to "lose" Randy, but soon John welcomed the constant company. Randy not only attended every one of John's classes and ate with him at lunchtime, he also went to football practice. After a few days, John asked the coach to make Randy the official manager responsible for the balls, tape, and water bottles. At the end of the football season, the team won the state championship, and John was awarded with a gold medal as the Most Valuable Player in the state. Randy was presented with a school letterman jacket. The team cheered as Randy put it on. It was the coolest thing that had ever happened to him; from that day forward, Randy never took it off. He slept in his jacket and wore it throughout each weekend.

Basketball season started, and John was also the captain and star of that team. At John's request, Randy was again named the manager. During the basketball season, they were still inseparable. Not only did John take Randy to special occasions—like dances as a joint escort for his girlfriend—but he also took Randy to the library to tutor him in his classes. As he tutored Randy, John became a much better student and made the honor roll for the first time in more than a year. The mentor program was unveiling itself as the most rewarding year of John's life.

Then tragedy struck in the middle of the state basketball tournament. Randy caught a virus and suddenly died of pneumonia. The funeral was held the day before the final championship game. John was asked to be one of the speakers. In his talk, John shared his thoughts about his deep, abiding friendship and respect for Randy. He told how Randy had been the one who had taught him about real courage, self-esteem, unconditional love, and the importance of giving 100 percent in everything he did. John dedicated the upcoming state finals game to Randy and concluded his remarks by stating that he was honored to have received the MVP award in football and the Leadership Plaque for being the captain of the basketball team. "But," John added, "the real leader of both the football and basketball teams was Randy, for he accomplished more with what he had than anyone I've ever met. Randy inspired all who knew him."

John walked from behind the podium, took off the irreplaceable, twenty-four-carat-gold state football MVP medallion that hung around his neck, leaned into the open casket, and placed it on Randy's chest. He placed his captain's plaque next to it.

Randy was buried in his letterman jacket, surrounded by John's cherished awards, as well as pictures and letters left by others who admired him. But this is not the end. The next day, John's team won the championship and presented the game ball to Randy's family. John went to college on a full athletic scholarship and graduated with a master's degree in education. Today John is a special education teacher and volunteers ten hours a week for the Special Olympics.

The Circus

When I was a young boy, my father and I were standing in line to buy tickets for the circus. Finally, there was only one family between us and the ticket counter. This family made a big impression on me. There were eight children, all probably under the age of twelve. You could tell they didn't have a lot of money. Their clothes were not expensive, but they were clean. The children were well behaved, all of them standing in line, two-by-two behind their parents, holding hands. They were excitedly jabbering about the clowns, elephants, and other acts they would see that night. We could tell they had never been to the circus before. It promised to be a highlight of their young lives.

The father and mother were at the head of the pack, standing proud as could be. The mother was holding her husband's hand, looking up at him as if to say, "You're my knight in shining armor." He was smiling and basking in pride, looking at her as if to reply, "You got that right."

The ticket lady asked the father how many tickets he wanted. He proudly responded, "Please let me buy eight children's tickets and two adult tickets so I can take my family to the circus."

The ticket lady quoted the price.

The man's wife let go of his hand. Her head dropped. The man's lip began to quiver. The father leaned a little closer and asked, "How much did you say?"

The ticket lady again quoted the price.

The man didn't have enough money.

How was he supposed to turn and tell his eight kids that he didn't have enough money to take them to the circus?

Seeing what was going on, my dad put his hand into his pocket, pulled out a twenty-dollar bill, and dropped it on the ground. (We were not wealthy in any sense of the word!) My father reached down, picked up the bill, tapped the man on the shoulder, and said, "Excuse me, sir, this fell out of your pocket."

The man knew what was going on. He wasn't begging for a handout, but certainly appreciated the help in a desperate, heartbreaking, embarrassing situation. He looked straight into my dad's eyes, took my dad's hand in both of his, squeezed tightly onto the twenty-dollar bill, and with his lip quivering and a tear streaming down his cheek, he replied, "Thank you, thank you, sir. This really means a lot to me and my family."

My father and I went back to our car and drove home. We didn't go to the circus that night, but we didn't go without.

The Art Collection

A father and son were very close and enjoyed adding valuable art pieces to their collection. Priceless works by Picasso, Van Gogh, Monet, and many other artists adorned the walls of the family estate. The son's trained eye and sharp business mind caused his widowed father to beam with pride as they dealt with art collectors around the world.

As winter approached, war engulfed the nation, and the young man left to serve his country. After only a few short weeks, his father received a telegram. His beloved son had died while rushing a fellow soldier to a medic. Distraught and lonely, the old man faced the future with anguish and sadness.

One morning, a knock on the door awakened the depressed old man. As he walked to the door, the masterpieces on the walls only reminded him that his son was not coming home. As he opened the door, he was greeted by a soldier with a large package in his hand. The soldier introduced himself to the man by saying, "I was a friend of your son. I was the one he was rescuing when he died. May I come in for a few moments? I have something to show you." As the two began to talk, the soldier told of how the man's son had told everyone of both his and his father's love of fine art. "I'm an artist," said the soldier, "and I want to give you this."

As the old man unwrapped the package, the paper gave way to reveal a portrait of the man's son. Though the world would never consider it the work of a genius, the painting featured the young man's face in striking detail. Overcome with emotion, the man thanked the soldier, promising to hang the picture above the fireplace.

A few hours later, after the soldier had departed, the old man set about his task. True to his word, the painting went above the fireplace, pushing aside thousands of dollars' worth of paintings.

As other stories of his son rescuing dozens of wounded soldiers continued to reach him, fatherly pride and satisfaction began to ease the grief. The painting of his son became his most prized possession, far eclipsing any interest in the pieces for which museums around the world clamored. He told his neighbors it was the greatest gift he had ever received.

The following spring, the old man became ill and passed away. The art world waited in anticipation for his paintings to be sold at an auction.

The appointed day soon arrived, and art collectors from around the world gathered to bid on some of the world's most spectacular paintings. Dreams would be fulfilled this day; greatness would be achieved as many would claim, "I now have the greatest collection."

The auction began with a painting that was not on any museum's list. It was the painting of the man's son. The auctioneer asked for an opening bid. The room was silent. "Who will open the bidding with one hundred dollars?" he asked. Minutes passed. No one spoke. From the back of the room came, "Who cares about that painting? It's just a picture of his son. Let's forget it and go on to the good stuff." More voices echoed in agreement.

"No, we have to sell this one first," replied the auctioneer. "Now, who will take the son?" Finally, a friend of the old man spoke. "Will you take ten dollars for the painting? That's all I have. I knew the boy, so I'd like to have it."

"I have ten dollars. Will anyone go higher?" called the auctioneer.

After more silence, the auctioneer said, "Going once, going twice. Gone."

The gavel fell. Cheers filled the room and someone exclaimed, "Now we can get on with it and start bidding on these treasures!"

The auctioneer looked at the audience and announced the auction was over. Stunned disbelief quieted the room. Someone spoke up and asked, "What do you mean it's over? We didn't come here for a picture of some old guy's son. What about all of these paintings? There are millions of dollars' worth of art here!"

The auctioneer replied, "It's very simple. According to the will of the father, whoever takes the son gets it all."

The Thermodynamics of Hell

The following is an actual question given on a University of Washington chemistry midterm. The answer by one student was so profound that the professor shared it with colleagues.

Bonus Question: Is hell exothermic (gives off heat) or endothermic (absorbs heat)?

Most of the students wrote proofs of their belief using Boyle's Law (gas cools off when it expands and heats up when it is compressed) or some variant. One student, however, wrote the following:

First, we need to know how the mass of hell is changing in time. So we need to know the rate that souls are moving into hell and the rate they are leaving. I think that we can safely assume that once a soul gets to hell, it will not leave. Therefore, no souls are leaving.

As for how many souls are entering hell, let's look at the different religions that exist in the world today. Some of these religions say that if you are not a member of their religion, you will go to hell. Since there are more than one of these religions and since people do not belong to more than one religion, we can project that all souls go to hell. With birth and death rates as they are, we can expect the number of souls in hell to increase exponentially.

Now, we look at the rate of change of the volume in hell because Boyle's Law states that in order for the temperature and pressure in hell to stay the same, the volume of hell has to expand proportionately as souls are added. This gives two possibilities:

1. If hell is expanding at a slower rate than the rate at which souls enter hell, then the temperature and pressure in hell will increase until all hell breaks loose.
2. Of course, if hell is expanding at a rate faster than the increase of souls in hell, then the temperature and pressure will drop until hell freezes over.

So which is it? If we accept the postulate given to me by Ms. Teresa Banyan during my freshman year, "It will be a cold day in hell before I sleep with you," and take into account the fact that I still have not succeeded in having sexual relations with her, then #2 cannot be true, and, thus, I am sure that hell is exothermic and will not freeze.

The student received the only "A" given!

Light the Fire Within

I am always inspired by the Olympic Games and emotionally moved by the opening ceremonies. The spirit of the 2002 Winter Games in Salt Lake City especially touched my heart—the Native Americans on horseback, the dancing to the drums. When they brought in the ripped, battered, and torn American flag that was flying on the World Trade Center on September 11, there wasn't a dry eye in the fifty-thousand-seat stadium. The lighting of the Olympic flame sent chills up and down my spine and added a giant crescendo to what would be one of the most significant experiences of my life.

On February 6, 2002, I was deeply honored and privileged to be one of the torchbearers who carried the Olympic flame. There were only 11,520 of us who carried the flame an average of two-tenths of a mile at a time, passing it from one to another across forty-six states. The flame was handed person to person until it was passed more than 13,500 miles on a journey that took a total of sixty-five days. Each of us runners proudly held the thirty-three-inch, three-and-a-half-pound butane-fired torch, and each of us had been nominated and selected because of our stories. There were cancer survivors and physically challenged people young and old. A high school student ran in front of his campus wearing the shoes of his brother who had been killed at that spot a week earlier.

I ran the torch on the sixty-third day and was blessed to be the final runner of the day, which meant I got to carry it one-half mile and light the cauldron in the back of the specially designed truck to transport the flame to the next city. I was so emotionally moved by the whole experience that tears flowed down my cheeks for most of my run. My personal story and experience is worth telling, but not here and now. The story I wish to share epitomizes the power of the flame and defines the motto engraved on every torch: "Light the Fire Within."

As each of us was notified that we had been selected to carry the torch, we received a white running suit (in our previously specified size) and a detailed account of when and where we would be running.

On the day of my run, all runners attended a special orientation, where it was pointed out with extreme emphasis that when we had our torch ignited by the oncoming torchbearer and his or her torch was immediately extinguished, that each of us, for that one moment in time, would be the keeper of the sacred Olympic flame; that for that brief moment, I would be the only one in the entire world holding and displaying the last pure sign of international world peace left on the planet! Wow! What a mind-boggling, awesome opportunity and responsibility.

The orientation was conducted by a young man and young woman in charge of the entire sixty-five-day torch relay. Their job was to make sure every runner showed up at his or her location so the relay never missed a beat. If there was a last-minute cancellation, they were equipped in the official van with extra running suits in every size to accommodate a last-minute replacement runner.

When one man with cancer received his letter stating that he had been nominated to carry the torch, he immediately put the date on his calendar. Against his doctor's advice, he trained to be in shape when the day came. His cancer spread, and his training threw him into a coma. The lady in charge of the relay was notified, and while she was arranging a replacement runner, the man miraculously came out of his two-week coma on the morning of his run. An ambulance delivered him to the pick-up point. He was assisted to the middle of the road with his torch to receive the flame from the oncoming runner, had his torch ignited and proudly ran his quarter-mile segment.

No one could believe it, and everyone cheered as they witnessed the inner strength exposed and supported by the spirit and power of the Olympic flame. As soon as the man lit the next runner's torch and his torch was extinguished, he collapsed in the road and was put back in the ambulance. Seconds later, he lapsed back into a coma and died soon after returning to the hospital. On one morning in Houston, Texas, a call came in that an elderly woman would not be able to make it for her relay segment. Scrambling to find a qualified substitute, the young woman in charge was driving the van down the route and passed by an elementary school. She immediately stopped and ran into the building. Frantically she introduced herself and asked the principal to help her. Who would she select to carry the Olympic Torch? A teacher, a counselor, an "A" student?

The young woman told the principal, "I need the child in your school who kids make fun of, who doesn't have a lot of friends and usually sits alone—the student who has a tough home life and struggles with his or her schoolwork." The principal's face lit up like a Christmas tree. "I have just the lad you're looking for!"

The principal introduced the young woman to a tiny, shoddy-looking fourth-grade boy. He was secretly outfitted in his very own official torch relay tracksuit, given a brief orientation, and escorted out of school to join the other relay runners in the van. No one in the school knew what was happening except that they were excused from class and assembled on the sides of the street in front of their school to join the thousands of other people already gathered, ready, and waiting to wave their flags and cheer on the lone torchbearer who would run right in front of them.

The relay van finally pulled up and stopped at the end of the road. The oncoming torch runner was greeted with screams and yells. Some onlookers were even moved to tears. As he drew near, the van door opened, and out into the street stepped the young fourth-grader all decked out in his white suit and holding the torch that was almost as big as he was. The torchbearer ignited his torch and the little lad began to jog.

The first sounds from his fellow students and school faculty members were moans and gasps of disbelief. Comments quickly turned negative: "How did he get out there? He must have stolen the torch! My wife's sister's dog's mother-in-law said he would never amount to a hill of beans!"

Although he could hear the mean-spirited, cutting comments, because of the orientation, this young lad fought back his tears of pain and insecurity, kept his head up, and held the torch with pride and dignity. As he ran, a schoolmate shouted out his name in disgust. But the mean comment didn't have a derogatory effect. The crowd embraced it as a positive and started chanting his name. The teachers and students couldn't believe it, but were caught up in the excitement and one by one joined in. As he ran past his now encouraging, cheering classmates and ignited the next torchbearer's torch, the crowd got louder and louder. Tears filled most of the faculty's eyes. As his flame was extinguished by the motorcycle policeman escorting him and he boarded the van to return back to his pickup point, it was explained to the onlookers that for that one moment in time, this little fourth-grader was the official ambassador of world peace; that he, though young and small, was for that brief time, one of the most important and significant people in the entire world.

Two days later, the young woman in charge of the relay received a handwritten FedEx letter from the principal. It simply read, "I trust you already know the power of the flame. I'm confident you already realize the self-fulfilling prophecy of the Olympic motto. But you have no idea what that one magical torch-running moment did to change the attitudes of my faculty and transform the tolerance level of my students. This one experience truly did 'Light the Fire Within.' Thank you. You have changed our school and our community forever. P.S. Billy no longer sits alone!"

In the next and subsequently following Olympic Games, let us rekindle our desire to help ourselves and others. Light the Fire Within and never ever forget the power of the flame!

Promises

A young Japanese boy was spending the weekend with his elderly grandfather. The rendezvous would take place at the train station, for the grandfather lived in a village on the other side of the mountain. The boy's parents dropped him off, hugged both of them good-bye, and drove away.

As the two of them waited in line to buy their tickets, the grandfather discovered that he had left his wallet on the previous train. He didn't have any money. It was cold and blizzardy, and he asked the ticket lady if she would loan him yen valuing fifty dollars. The grandfather promised he would pay her back later that night.

Because of the Japanese culture's deep and abiding respect for its elders, the ticket lady believed the grandfather and paid for their tickets.

An hour later, they arrived in the village. They walked fifteen minutes through the horrible weather and finally entered the cottage. Hungry, tired, and soaking wet, the grandfather went to his drawer and retrieved some money. "Let's go," he said. His grandson rebutted, "But Grandfather, I'm starving and we're going back to the train station in three days. Why can't you just pay her back then? It will cost you the price of two more round-trip tickets to go now, just to pay back two one-way passes." Putting on a dry overcoat and handing his grandson a wool blanket for comfort, the eighty-year-old grandfather put his arm around his grandson's shoulders and taught him the lesson of the ages. "Son, we must get there tonight before the counter closes and she goes home. This is not about money. This is about honor. I gave her my word, and we must always keep our promises!"

A Swimmer's Glory

Michael Swenson loved to swim. In fact, every night after school he would go to the community pool and swim lap after lap just for pure enjoyment. As time went on, Michael reached the age when he really needed some attention and recognition. And how do we get recognition? Usually by doing something we are good at.

In Michael's case, he decided to enter a swimming race. Ironically, the following day an ad appeared in the newspaper announcing a local meet. Michael entered and continued to practice. It was a ten-mile race across a lake. With only four weeks to prepare, Michael intensified his workouts.

Race day finally came, and to Michael's astonishment, hundreds of contestants had entered. On top of this pressure, thousands of people showed up to cheer for their favorite contender.

Instructions were given, the swimmers were lined up, and the gun went off to start the race. Michael's preparation and hard work paid off. At the five-mile mark he had a commanding lead. But then fatigue struck, and fatigue makes cowards of us all. Negative thoughts began flooding Michael's head. *What am I trying to prove? I can't make it,* Michael rationalized. *I'll quit now but learn from this so I can win next time.*

As Michael slowed down, the second-place swimmer started to make his move. He swam to within one hundred yards of Michael at the eight-mile mark. But Michael fought back. His second wind kicked in, and he was able to put the negative thoughts aside and push himself to greatness. He decided that he wanted this victory, this glory. At the nine-mile mark, the second-place swimmer was now only thirty yards behind him. Michael knew it and pushed himself even harder.

With only five yards to go, the second-place contestant passed Michael and won the race. Both swimmers collapsed and lay in the sand, grasping for breath.

Then something interesting happened. All the spectators congratulated the winner for his excellence but immediately turned their attention to Michael. *Why?* he wondered. After all, he hadn't won. A lady passing by who didn't see the race and couldn't see the contestants was also confused.

She tapped a man on the shoulder and asked, "Why are they making such a big deal of this guy? He didn't win!"

The man turned to her and replied, "Because Michael would have easily won if he had two arms!"

Making Memories

It was the holiday season, with the "big three"—Halloween, Thanksgiving, and Christmas—just ahead. My father was battling cancer at that time. Afraid that he wouldn't be around for Christmas, I wanted to make that year extra special. I thought the perfect gift was a grandfather clock, hand-built by me. It was one of the things he had always wanted but could never afford. Although I had not built anything of that complexity, I felt it would not only make my dad proud of me, but it would give him something from me that he could treasure.

I purchased a magnificent self-assembly kit and immediately devoted my time to the overwhelming task of putting it together.

Every day after work, I went to my brother's house to secretly work on the clock. Three hours a day, six days a week, I labored all alone, trying to figure out those complicated instructions. As it started to take form, the anticipation and internal excitement were almost too much to bear. I was really proud and couldn't help visualizing how surprised, appreciative, and amazed my dad would surely be when he unwrapped the masterpiece. On October 10, I finally finished the clock and wrapped it up with a big red bow, ready to be delivered in a couple of months on Christmas Eve. The next morning I left on a trip to Washington.

Two days later the phone rang in my hotel room. It was my brother. "Dad just died," he cried.

That was a sad and brutal Christmas for me. Mom had a gorgeous Christmas tree. There were gifts galore. And there in the corner of my mother's living room stood the tall, solid-oak grandfather clock that I had spent sixty-three hours building. But there was no Dad! The presents meant nothing, and the clock meant nothing in comparison to the loss of my dad.

Not a day goes by that I don't regret the time I spent on that clock, now knowing that I should have spent those final, most sacred hours—all sixty-three of them—at my father's side. Most people use people and love things when we should love people and use things. What a fool I was to think a "thing" would make him happy. Things don't make people happy. Time spent together with loved ones does!

Attitude Is Everything

When my son, Spencer, was in the first grade, he was having trouble saying his Rs. We thought it was cute until one day Spencer came home with tears in his eyes. I asked what was wrong, and he softly said, "Mom, the kids at school ah making fun of me. They say I can't say my ahs vewee good."

"What should we do about it?" I asked.

"The nuse lady said my attitude is evweething. All I have to do is just pwactice." Every day for two weeks, Spencer stood in front of the mirror before and after school and worked and worked until he could say his Rs perfectly.

In the third grade, he entered competitive sports. He was ready for the ordeal— I wasn't. I thought he still looked newly hatched and terribly vulnerable. "Today I have to stay after school again and practice track," he announced one day. "Why don't you come watch me?"

Of course I went. I watched, and my heart ached because he was trying so hard with such discouraging results. From birth, one leg was three inches shorter than the other, and he had great difficulty running. Consequently, he was a high jumper, who with one strong leg flung himself through the air, often landing on the bar. Although he became scratched and battered from his fifteen attempts, he relentlessly pursued his goal.

"Haven't you had enough?" I asked in a feeble attempt to protect him from further failure. With tears in his eyes he softly answered, "The kids make fun of me and say I'm not too good at track, but the coach said I can't quit; it's a league rule."

On the next try, he succeeded in clearing the bar.

At the end of the track season, I thought he had had enough last-place finishes to last a lifetime. To the contrary, he excitedly proposed, "I think I'll try out for the Little League baseball team. Maybe I'm good at baseball." He wasn't. Not only could he not run, but he couldn't see the ball. He wore thick Coke-bottle glasses.

Each evening, he returned to me exhausted, never complaining about what he couldn't do. He was tired but always had a smile.

"I missed every fly that came my way," he said one night.

"That's too bad," I sympathized. I put a comforting hand on his shoulder and noticed several bruises on his chest.

"What are these spots?" I asked.

He looked down. "Oh those. That's where the ball hit me."

"My goodness! Shouldn't you duck when you're about to get hit?"

His eyes widened, saddened. "Mom, I wasn't supposed to get hit."

"Why didn't you catch it?" I persisted.

Spencer's countenance changed and his head dropped. "That's what I was trying to do."

That night I cried myself to sleep, wondering if and when he would ever really succeed. The next day I picked him up from practice, and he had his new uniform. He ran to the car with the blue and gold jersey slung over his shoulder and a smile that lit up his face like a Christmas tree.

"I got a uniform," he announced. "There were only twelve of them. Most guys didn't get one. This was the last uniform, and the coach gave it to me. He said I'd earned it."

"Way to go," I said. It was wonderful to see him so happy.

The benchwarming period began after that, and although he never missed a practice or a game, I lost interest. Rationalizing that I had something better to do than just sit on a hard bleacher and watch my son sit there, I stopped going. Spencer pleaded for me to cancel my Friday evening date and come to his final game. I arrived late but still in time to see him play. I guess his persistence had finally gotten to the coach and he put him in. In the sixth inning, which was the second to the last inning, the ball was hit his way. Spencer hobbled as fast as he could but missed it. Three more times he missed it, and the other team started catching up. Then when it was his turn to bat, he struck out. Each mistake was announced over the loudspeaker. I was mortified and embarrassed, but somehow Spencer was not. After his poor performance, I thought for sure Spencer would be pulled from the game. It was close, and they needed a victory to win the championship. To everyone's surprise, the coach yelled to the end of the bench, "Williams, you're back in."

As Spencer walked past the bleachers, he looked up at me and the other parents and, with his patented positivity reassuredly cautioned, "Whoa, Mom, we are only ahead by one run and I don't know if even I can hold them off with only one inning to play!"

We laughed. He was dead serious! No one seemed to worry, though, because this time, Spencer was put in right field where no balls had been hit all game long.

There were two quick hits with the winning run now on first base. Then two quick outs. The third hit came Spencer's way. I saw the coach wince and cover his eyes. The ball sailed right into Spencer's glove. We stood to cheer until he collided with another player. He lay motionless. The other player got up and screamed that Spencer's nose was gushing blood. "I think he's dead!" he shouted. "You'd better come quick." With the apparent winning run crossing home plate and the ballpark hushed in concerned silence, the coach jogged his way out of the dugout to administer first aid. Suddenly Spencer raised his hand in the air. The ball had stayed in his glove. The umpire yelled, "You're out," and our bleachers erupted into a long-cheering, standing ovation. Spencer's team had won the game! The coach stopped walking. He couldn't believe it. No one could. With tears in his eyes, he proudly started to clap. Then in a spontaneous eruption of sportsmanship, the other team started to clap. Although they had just lost the game, one by one the opposing team members stood. Within a minute, the other fans, the two umpires, the other team's coaches, and every player on both teams were on their feet cheering for this eight-year-old hero.

My Spencer is now thirteen years old. It has been five years since that amazing day, and I've never missed another one of his extracurricular activities. In fact, I've stopped procrastinating, changed my previous life perception from half empty to half full, stopped whining about my job layoff, got more education and training, which landed me more fulfilling employment in a new job, and have never missed another day of work or a day at the gym since then. How could I when I now know that "Attitude is everything!"

Self-Worth

Jillene

Her name was Jillene Jones. She told me it was Portuguese for "awesome woman" and she was right. She was wonderful! I wanted to go out with her more than anything in the world. I was somewhat insecure and didn't want her to turn me down, so to protect my heart and ego, I asked some of her friends if she would go out with me. They all said yes. I got my confidence up, practiced my voice to make sure it was low and breathy, and phoned her. I asked her to a concert two weeks away. She said yes!

My plan was to get her to fall in love with me. I didn't think Jillene could possibly like me just the way I was, so I started asking around to find out what she did like. I was willing to change anything about myself to get Jillene to fall madly in love with me. I was willing to sell out and compromise my personal authenticity just to reel her in.

I spent the next fourteen days researching Jillene. I discovered her favorite color was peach. What a drag. Peach is a popular color now, but in college it was definitely uncool for a guy to wear peach. You just didn't do it. But it was Jillene's favorite color. I wanted her to fall madly in love with me. Suddenly, it was my favorite color. Interesting how that works, eh? And no, I didn't just buy one peach shirt—I bought five peach shirts. I was thinking long-term relationship!

More research revealed Jillene's favorite men's cologne—an exotic-sounding substance that stunk so bad my nose hairs threatened my life. When I splashed it on, my eyes fogged up, my ears tried to bleed, and my eyes started to sting! But it didn't matter. It was Jillene's favorite cologne. Suddenly it was my favorite cologne. No, I didn't buy the small, date-size bottle. I bought the huge forever-relationship-size bottle. It cost me a bloomin' fortune!

I did more research and discovered Jillene's favorite music. I liked all kinds of music, but hers was really different. Heavy, heavy metal. Brutal loud stuff. Sometimes I think the only reason they call it heavy metal is because the lead singer sounds like he dropped something heavy on his foot! And to think they wrote this all by themselves! Whoa! Give them a Grammy! Yeah, I bought a CD. Suddenly, heavy metal had become my favorite kind of music. It's interesting how insecurity works.

Two weeks went by. It was finally date night. It was time to take Jillene to the concert. I took my research seriously and put on a peach shirt, drenched myself in the cologne, and went to pick up Jillene. I stunk so bad that the flowers on her front porch began to wilt.

Jillene answered the door, and all my preparation paid off. "Oh, my gosh! I can't believe it. Nobody wears peach. Peach is my favorite color." She gave me a hug. "Oh my gosh," she continued, "this is my favorite smell—my favorite cologne."

I coughed and choked, "Me too. I can't believe how many things we have in common." She smiled and said, "I know, I know."

I walked her to the car, opened her door, and walked around the car gagging for oxygen. I then popped in the CD and played her favorite song. As we pulled out of her driveway she leaped over the console and started singing (or screaming) to the beat, and head banging up and down in heavy-metal contortions. I joined her, nodding my head up and down until I accidentally hit her nose on my forehead. As her nose started to bleed, she yelled, "Wow, you're a great slam dancer. This is my favorite band."

I yelled over the loud music, "Me too!" We pulled onto the street and headed for the concert.

Jillene fell madly in love with me exactly as I had planned. In fact, she fell in love with me for two weeks. But something happened. I got sick and tired of being Jillene Jones. I was born to be me! I was born into this world to discover myself and become a unique person that I could love and respect twenty-four hours a day—every day. And yet I had just sold out to win over a woman! And how many women sell out to win over a bloomin' man? We change our hairstyles, health habits, high expectations, moral standards, style of clothing, cologne, and tastes in music just so an individual or some cliquish group or club will welcome us and accept us with open arms.

After two weeks, I got sick and tired of being Jillene. I was born to be me. So, I gave the peach shirts to my sister. I threw the cologne away. (My trash cans smelled so badly every dog within thirty miles of my home had brain damage!) I then got rid of her musical noise and started listening to my own tunes. I even started doing the old favorite things I had once enjoyed. And do you know what? It turned out Jillene Jones didn't like that me. When I finally started to be real, we were completely different and she didn't like me. But that's okay because I like me. I have to like and love myself before I can honestly like and love someone else. Do you like and love yourself? If not, why? And if not now, when?

It's What's on the Inside

On a spring day in New York's Central Park, a balloon salesman was busy trying to sell his balloons. In order to gain the attention of those walking in the park, from time to time he would release a brightly colored balloon and let it rise into the sky.

On this sunny afternoon, a little African American girl approached him. She was shy and had a poor self-image. She had been watching the man and had a question for him.

"Mister, if you let a black balloon go, will it rise too?" The balloon salesman knew what the girl was asking.

"Sweetheart," he explained. "It doesn't matter what color the balloon is. It's not what's on the outside that makes it rise; it's what's on the inside that makes it go up."

Needed?

I was speaking to members of Our Primary Purpose (OPP), a highly acclaimed program for chemically dependent teenagers in Des Moines, Iowa. At the third meeting, just for parents, a mother shared her story:

Her twenty-year-old son John (who incidentally was not enrolled in the OPP program) was handsome and talented, a good citizen, a good student, a good musician, and a gifted athlete. He also had a lovely girlfriend and seemed to have no problems. One day he stopped talking as much as he usually did. Thirty days passed, and his conversation dwindled to nothing. He was depressed, and his parents and girlfriend continually told him that they loved him. He knew that they loved him, and he expressed his love for them. Everyone was concerned about his well-being and wondered what they could say or do to help him, since saying "I love you" obviously wasn't enough to improve the situation.

John finally made a move. He locked himself in the cellar. Although he was down in the dim dampness for three days without food, he continued to acknowledge his parents' love for him and his love for them. But his depression deepened, and his loved ones were convinced suicide was imminent. Healthcare professionals were brought in, but the counseling, kindness, caring, and love did not help.

On the third day of John's isolation, the local high school football coach (who didn't know what was going on in John's life) called his home to talk to him. John's mother said John was busy and took a message at the coach's request. Then she went to the cellar door and called down the stairs, "John, Coach Ivers just phoned. He said that his players voted last night on who they wanted as their assistant coach. They said you were the greatest Pop Warner football coach they had ever had and now they think they can win the state championship if you help coach them. Coach Ivers said they need you—he needs you! He said if you're interested, you should be at football practice at 2:45 this afternoon."

Do you know what happened? Sure you do! John came out of the cellar and went to practice. He accepted the coaching job, and by the time he came home from his first practice, he had snapped out of his depression. He once again felt needed, wanted, and important, and he was back to his old self.

Do You Shun Competition?

Competition is the economic system America is based on. Capitalism exists and thrives on this simple principle.

Mr. Ling owned a dry-cleaning store that had been in the family for years. Then a developer came along and wanted to push Mr. Ling out of his spot to make room for a new shopping mall. Mr. Ling did not know how to do anything else for a living. He didn't want to lose this store, and he made it clear to the developer he was going to stay put.

The conflict escalated as the developer built the shopping mall around Mr. Ling's establishment. To get even, the developer put dry-cleaning shops on both sides of Mr. Ling to drive him out of business. Most would have quit, but not Mr. Ling.

The Ling family hadn't been in business for so many years without knowing how to compete and survive. To combat the competition, Mr. Ling made a giant sign and hung it above the entrance of his store. After he hung the sign, Mr. Ling had more business than ever. What did the sign say? THIS WAY TO MAIN ENTRANCE.

There is always a way to survive. When we rise to the level of our competition, we become better.

Like Mr. Ling, you might find it hard, but only those who compete are going to survive, thrive, and succeed.

Painful Preparation

The incredible courage shown by tiny, tenacious Kari Strug in the 1996 Olympic Games in Atlanta, Georgia, reminds us all about the powerful cliché "Proper prior planning prevents poor performance." It also reminds us that both physical *and* mental toughness are required to be a champion.

A few years ago, I went to a workout session of the University of Utah women's gymnastic team. I learned why they win consistently.

Her name was Missy Marlowe, and she eventually competed on the U.S. Olympic gymnastics team in 1988. She was also named one of the prestigious top six—one of the six best male and female athletes in the United States—and received the Broderick Award as the NCAA Outstanding Female Athlete of the Year.

When I first saw her, Missy was a young freshman on the uneven parallel bars, trying to execute a difficult maneuver. I watched her crash to the mat ten times in a row. After the tenth fall, she sobbed and limped away, but it didn't stop her. She came back, and I watched her fall four more times, each time smashing hard into the mat. Finally, on the fifteenth try, Missy spun off the bar, reached out, and completed the maneuver.

Coach Marsden told me afterward that every new girl goes through the same thing to learn each one of the many difficult moves required to win meets and please judges. Nobody clapped that day. There were no cameras to record her victory. But her face showed personal satisfaction. And when she eventually won the national championship that year in the all-around competition, the hard work, sacrifice, and painful endurance were all worth it.

Would you have quit on the first crash? The tenth? The fourteenth? How many of us would have realized that just one more attempt would make the difference between failure and success?

Any great achievement in life requires hours of lonely, deliberate preparation and work. Don't make the mistake of thinking that athletes, artists, doctors, attorneys, writers, or actors didn't spend years learning how to perform in their areas of expertise. You can be sure they paid their dues in time, effort, and solitude. They were convinced, however, that there's no gain without pain.

Discipline

Responsibility brings freedom and freedom provides opportunity. That's the principle of self-discipline.

Self-discipline sounds like some kind of punishment you administer to yourself. It really means you are in control of your actions and the outcome—at least to some degree.

Self-discipline means avoiding outside discipline by doing the right thing. Arabian horses are a perfect example of the kind of self-control each of us is capable of achieving. These magnificent horses with intelligent eyes, well-formed heads, and flowing manes and tails win many championships because of their stamina and courage.

While they are all hearty specimens, some horses stand above the others for endurance and intelligence. To determine which they are, trainers teach them to drink only when they hear a whistle. Once they have learned to obey, they are placed in a corral under the hot sun until they are parched. Then water is brought and placed outside the corral out of their reach, forcing them to wait even longer. Finally, a gate is opened, and most of them stampede for the trough to drink with reckless abandon. Only a few stand poised with pride, holding their heads erect, and don't give in to the terrible craving. Only when they hear the whistle do they allow themselves to drink. The ones who obey and resist the urge to drink are reserved for special training. The other steeds are led away.

So it is with humans. The mark of a champion is not on the outside, but somewhere deep inside, where self-control resides. To gain control of yourself and become self-disciplined is the second step to becoming successful. First, see yourself as a conqueror. Then discipline yourself to become one.

Unfortunately, many folks who see themselves as champions are not willing to put in the extra effort and self-imposed discipline to become winners. Consequently, they lose out to those with restraint.

Trials

One day a man, who was not a believer in God, stopped at the little gorge to talk to his blacksmith friend, who had recently become a believer in God. Sympathizing with the blacksmith in some of his current trials, the man said, "It seems strange to me that so much affliction should come to you, just at the time when you have become a believer. I can't help wondering why it is."

The blacksmith answered, "You see the raw iron I have here to make into horseshoes. You know what I do with it? I take a piece and heat it in the fire until it is red, almost white with the heat. Then I hammer it unmercifully to shape it as I know it should be shaped. Then I plunge it into a pail of cold water to temper it. Then I heat it again and hammer it some more. And this I do until it is finished.

"But sometimes I find a piece of iron that won't stand up under this treatment. The heat and the hammering and the cold water are too much for it and it fails in the process." He pointed to a heap of scrap iron that was near the door of his shop. "When I get a piece that cannot take the temperatures and hammering, I throw it out on the scrap heap. It will never be good for anything."

He finished his answer. "I know that God has been holding me in the fires of affliction, and I have felt life's hammer upon me. But I don't mind, if only He can bring me to what I should be. Try me in any way you wish, Lord, just don't throw me on the scrap heap!"

Potential

In high school, we had a couple of girls' choice dances each year. I went to every one of them. Never once did I go with the girl of my dreams. Never once did I ever go with a girl that I really wanted to go with. Why? I always went with the girl who asked me first. Why? Because of an experience I have had many times before. Guys, you can relate—girls, please listen.

One of the worst things a girl can do is turn someone down when he asks you to dance. You have the right to say no to a guy and that's cool. You need to say no in various circumstances, and you know what I'm talking about. But for a simple dance? C'mon.

Our dances were always held in the gymnasium. A band or a DJ would provide the tunes. Nobody ever danced the first couple of dances. Everyone just stayed on the perimeter checking things out. The boys were always on one side of the gym sitting in the stands scoping for love. All the girls sat on the other side when I was in high school, waiting for love. Now the girls are also scoping for love! They have even perfected the technique to where they focus on exactly what they want. "Whoa, I want to be his girlfriend. He looks like he even has a job!"

I was sitting in the stands with my friends when all of a sudden, I focused in on one lady. She was awesome. I thought that was my chance to show my friends how wonderful I thought I was. So, I stood up, cinched up my belt, flexed my neck (that's important), and did a long swagger, as-if-I-had-sat-on-something-hot-walk across the dance floor and said to her, "Excuse me, would you like to dance?" She turned and looked me square in the eye and said, "No." That was the longest walk back! When I got back to the other side of the gym with my friends, they started to slag, "What's wrong, Clark? Did she turn you down?"

I blurted, "No, she doesn't even speak English. I don't know what happened."

"Yeah, right," they laughed.

Because this happened to me so many times, when these girls asked me to go to the girls' choice dances, I didn't have the heart to turn them down. Their feelings were important—I knew exactly what it felt like to be rejected. So I said yes. Let's face it. These girls were not the beauty queens in my high school. These girls were the wallflowers.

No, on date night, I did not pick them up at 6:30 PM and take them home at 7:00 PM. I did all the things I would do if I were on my dream date: polish my shoes, rent a tuxedo if it was appropriate, wash Dad's car. At the dance, sure my friends were cruel. I was out on the dance floor dancing the night away, and my friends were slipping me coupons for contact lenses. "Man, you've got some eyesight problems." Another poked, "She's uglier than a mud fence. She could make a freight train take a dirt road. What are you doing?" Still another chided, "Take her to school and get an A on your science project." Boy these guys were cold!

At my five-year high school reunion, I learned the true definition of a word I had never really discussed before. Our whole lives we hear from parents and coaches and teachers, "You have so much potential." But what does it really mean?

When I walked into my five-year high school reunion, Corie Van Groll, a great friend from high school, ran up to me. She said, "Come here," and we started walking to the corner toward a round table. Sitting behind the table were four of the most beautiful women I have ever seen in my entire life. I might be crazy, but I'm not blind! My friend Corie asked, "Do you remember Gina? Do you remember Leah? Do you remember Kimberly and Marie?" These were four of the "wallflowers" that I had gone to the girls' choice dances with in high school! As I got closer, all I could think was, *Wow—what have you been eating?* I thought they ought to call Jane Fonda and tell her they were making their own exercise videos.

As I caught my breath and sat down to talk to these ladies, I discovered the importance of the word *potential*. These four women were not only beautiful on the outside, they were beautiful on the inside—where it matters most. So many of us get so caught up in being popular and cool in high school that we stop focusing on the things that outlast high school that will give us solid relationships, a secure job, and a meaningful future in the sixty years after high school graduation. We put so much emphasis on what seems to matter at the moment that we sell out what will matter for a lifetime.

To see the overweight homecoming queen and one of the loser basketball stars captain still hanging out with their dilapidated clique still telling each other lies about how wonderful they all are, and then to contrast them with former "plain Janes," who all along had their acts together on the inside, was an experience to remember. It put time and the years in college in proper perspective. Clearly these four women were the most solid, attractive, educated, sophisticated, well-rounded, beautiful people at the reunion!

Full Contact

At a full-contact karate meet in which a friend of mine competed, I was asked to hold two one-inch-thick boards out in front of me as my friend, Todd Peterson, attempted to break through them to demonstrate his punching power. I braced myself firmly for his effort and held the boards at arm's length. Todd hit the boards as hard as he could. WHAP! His hand landed with a thud.

The boards didn't break, but his knuckle did. I had practiced this routine with Todd before, and I had seen him break one board of this thickness, but never two. I thought he might give up, but giving up was not in Todd's nature. Quickly he punched again, this time breaking the boards on the third effort.

As I walked off the stage, I asked Todd what had gone wrong. He quickly replied, "I made a great mistake, Dan. Instead of looking through the boards at your chest, I looked at the boards. To do it right, you have to imagine a point past the point of impact."

The lesson is a good one for all of us.

If all we ever see are the hurdles in our way, we will never reach our destination. Look past the obstacles in your life, not at them. You only get stopped when you take your sights off the goal! As Todd found out, getting to the finish line may involve pain, even broken bones and broken dreams. So see the goal clearly, make full contact with life, break through every barrier, and don't give up until you make the dream come true.

Inspirational

Pay Attention

Jason came from a good family with two loving parents, two brothers, and a sister. They were all successful academically and socially. They lived in a posh neighborhood. Jason had everything a boy could desire. But he was always into some kind of mischief. He wasn't a bad kid who caused trouble, but he always wound up in the thick of bad things.

In first grade, Jason was labeled Special Ed. They tried to keep him out of the regular classes. In middle school, he was the "misfit troublemaker." In high school, although never officially tested, Jason was tagged with having attention deficit/hyperactivity disorder (ADHD). More often than not, his teachers kicked him out of class. His first report card had one C and all Ds.

One Sunday, the family was enjoying brunch at the country club when a teacher stopped and said, "Jason is doing so well these days. We're pleased and delighted."

"You must be mixing us up with another family," said the father. "Our Jason is worthless. He is always in trouble. We are so embarrassed and just can't figure out why."

As the teacher walked away, the mother remarked, "You know, honey, come to think of it, Jason hasn't been in trouble for a month. He's even been going to school early and staying late. I wonder what's up?"

The second nine-week grading period was finally up. As usual, Jason's mom and dad expected low grades and unsatisfactory marks in behavior. Instead, he achieved four As, three Bs, and honors in citizenship. His parents were baffled.

"Who did you sit by to get these grades?" his dad asked sarcastically.

"I did it all myself," Jason humbly answered.

Perplexed, and still not satisfied, the parents took Jason back to school to meet with the principal. He assured them that Jason was doing very well.

"We have a new guidance counselor, and she seems to have touched your son in a special way," he said. "His self-esteem is much better, and he's doing great this term. I think you should meet her."

When the trio approached the counselor, the woman had her head down. It took a moment for her to notice she had visitors. When she did, she leaped to her feet and began gesturing with her hands.

"What's this?" asked Jason's father indignantly. "Sign language? Why, she can't even hear."

"That's why she's so great," said Jason, jumping in between them. "She does more than hear, Dad. She listens!"

Miss America

One five-year-old wanted to be Miss America. She started to pursue her dream by enrolling in piano lessons. She also took voice lessons. But her dream and pursuit of musical excellence almost came to a screeching halt when she was eleven years old. A serious car accident left her physically challenged. She would never walk again.

For ten months, she wore a total body cast. When the cast came off, she could walk but only with a severe limp. She had a hundred stitches on her face as a result of the accident.

But she had a dream, so she continued on. At the age of seventeen, through hard work and undying faith, her leg miraculously healed, and she tried out for her first county beauty pageant. She lost, not even finishing in the top ten. The next year, she entered again and didn't make the five finalists. On the third try, she won the county pageant, but lost in the state pageant. The fourth year, she again won her county contest, but again lost by a landslide at the state level. The fifth year, at age twenty-two, she not only won locally, but finally won the state contest and became Miss Mississippi.

More than 75 million television viewers watched teary-eyed Cheryl Pruitt gracefully walk down the runway to be crowned Miss America. In all the glitz and glamour of that special night, in front of the lights, the American public didn't realize that the elegant, talented, articulate young woman almost didn't make it to Atlantic City at all.

It wasn't just a pretty face, a particular evening dress, or a smile that got her there. It was heart and soul and a relentless pursuit of personal excellence.

The Magic in Us All

The Los Angeles Lakers and the Philadelphia 76ers were battling it out in a seven-game NBA championship series. In the sixth game, the great and overpowering center for the Lakers, Kareem Abdul Jabbar, was hurt. He had a migraine and a torn ankle. He wasn't able to make the trip to Philadelphia for the final championship game.

It was a devastating blow to the Lakers. The players lost hope of winning the championship. But instead of making excuses, the Lakers' head coach decided to make some adjustments. He knew they were winners and that they'd come too far to lose.

The coach, Pat Riley, took a twenty-year-old rookie and moved him from his guard position to center. That adjustment was tough enough for the six-foot-eight guard, but when he went up against Darryl Dawkins—a mass of muscle and intimidation who shattered backboards and opposing centers just for kicks, and who stood three inches taller—the rookie was terrified.

That young player's name was Earvin "Magic" Johnson, and he showed his genius that night. He scored forty-two points, grabbed fifteen rebounds, and earned the Most Valuable Player trophy for leading the Lakers to victory.

Earvin Johnson is another example of the magic we all have within. We can all rise to the occasion when the need is there.

Cornerstones

Too often, we hear speakers, trainers, and organizational leaders say, "You've got to think outside the box. We must think outside the lines." My question is, "What if the answers are still in the box?" What's true is still true, and what's right is always right when it comes to sales, customer service, leadership, management, and living life to its fullest. To succeed at anything, we must become brilliant at the basics.

There is nothing more basic or fundamental than music. There are only twelve notes in music. Some argue there are really only seven, i.e., A,B,C,D,E,F,G. But what about the five minor notes, the half-steps, the little things that make a big difference? Counting all of the notes, there are twelve, and they were discovered way before Beethoven, B.B. King, or Garth Brooks came along. The same twelve notes that are used to write a number one hit song are the same notes used to write a lousy one that never gets recorded. The only difference between one song and another is the order in which those twelve notes fall, and the timing and spacing in between the notes. Classical, rhythm and blues, jazz, hip hop, country, and heavy metal are all using the same twelve notes. Therefore, the only difference between a great song and a lousy song, the only difference between a great songwriter and a lousy songwriter, is Passion, Creativity, and Imagination. Similarly, the only difference between a great, successful catering executive and a lousy, non-effective catering executive is Passion, Creativity, and Imagination.

You have to stretch before you strengthen. All the strengthening occurs in the area past the point of discomfort. We cannot succeed alone; we cannot become the very best we can be by ourselves. We need a "physical therapist" of the mind and heart to stretch us and take us to the places we cannot take ourselves. Leaders who do this are the executives who have Passion, Creativity, and Imagination, and it only takes one in an entire organization to transform everyone else around them.

One moment in time can change forever. We need to live our lives, personally and professionally, so that when our friends, families, and co-workers are away from us, they can honestly say, "I like me best when I'm with you. I want to see you again." We don't always have to have all the answers, or even know how to fix what is broken. We do need to know that we are there for one another through thick and thin and that as we strive to bring more Passion, Creativity, and Imagination into our lives, we are there emotionally holding each others' hands.

Henry Aaron

Henry Aaron broke Babe Ruth's career record of 714 home runs to become the greatest long-ball hitter in baseball history. He now holds the record for the most career homers.

Henry Aaron didn't start at the top. In fact, he didn't even play baseball in high school because his school didn't have a team. Instead, he considered himself a bookworm. It wasn't until he was in his early twenties that he finally caught baseball fever and decided to pursue a professional career in sports. At the time, there were few African Americans playing in major-league baseball. So he joined a semipro team called the Indianapolis Clowns of the Negro American League.

Henry played for two hundred dollars a month, waiting and praying for his first big break. Then a Milwaukee Braves scout spotted him and signed him to the "big time." When Henry stepped up to the batter's box for the first time in his major-league career, he was understandably nervous. There were two outs. The pressure was on. Thousands of eyes waited for him to perform. To cap it off, the opposing team catcher sneered at Henry as he came to the plate. As Henry held the bat with a cross-handed grip, the catcher sneered, "Hey, kid, you're holding the bat wrong. You're supposed to see the label."

Henry turned and looked straight into the catcher's eyes. "I didn't come here to read," he said. "I came here to hit." With that, he drilled the next pitch into the outfield for a single and laughed his way to first base.

Henry Aaron became one of baseball's all-time greats. And from firsthand experience, he understands the saying, "Believe in yourself. At times, you're the only one who will."

Player of the Year

Anemia is a condition in which a person's blood is deficient in red blood cells and total volume. If it is not corrected, it can result in constant weakness, fatigue, or even death. That is what a doctor told a young boy in Worthing, Texas, back in 1971. The doctor also told him he would never be able to compete in sports. But that young boy had a dream to play football and was determined to prove the doctor wrong.

In his freshman year of high school, he was told he was too small and weak to play. So he became the team manager. But after everyone else had left, he stayed and ran laps and wind sprints. He struggled to lift weights. His sophomore year, he told his father his goal was to make the team and get a uniform like the rest of the guys. He got a uniform but never played. He stayed after every practice and, all alone, worked out and ran.

In his junior year, he told his father he wanted to get into at least one game. The last game of the season, his team was far ahead, and he was sent in to play the whole fourth quarter. After the game he told his father he wanted to play in every game his senior year and earn a scholarship to college. He got a chance to go to Baylor University. After injuries to three other linebackers in his first year, he was moved to starting linebacker. In his junior and senior years, he was the unanimous choice for All-American. He signed a pro contract as a second-round draft pick of the Super Bowl Champion Chicago Bears.

Mike Singletary wound up the best middle linebacker in the National Football League, anchored one of the best defenses in NFL history, and was honored as NFL Defensive Player of the Year. If he had listened to all the limitations other people had placed on him, Mike would never have reached the goals he set for himself. Do what is inside of you, regardless of what others say you can't do.

Absorb the Bumps

Bill Latimer was one of the greatest athletes in America and an intense competitor. As a student at the University of Utah, he was a star on the tennis team and one of the best competitive skiers. Things were going well for Bill. In fact, things couldn't have been better—until Bill had a skiing accident and the doctor had to amputate his left leg just below the knee.

Needless to say, Bill was devastated. However, he realized if he continued to compete and compare himself to others, he would feel handicapped and incapable. But if he looked at what he now had to work with, he could turn the negative label of "handicapped" into a positive opportunity to overcome a physical challenge.

And Bill was a guy who had sought out physical challenges his entire life.

With this newfound understanding of self-competition, Bill promised himself that he would never let anyone see him walk with a limp. He vowed that he would not let this accident stop him from competing.

Bill had two kinds of artificial legs made for him. One had a foot with a convex bottom and a rocking-chair effect, so he does not limp when he walks. No one knows he has an artificial leg unless he wears shorts. With this leg, Bill still plays tournament tennis and wins. He's an amazing racquetball player and swims long-distance marathon races.

The other artificial leg he had made is constructed so that he can wear a ski boot. Bill is still a fantastic powder skier, but sometimes it's hard for him to negotiate the bumps. One day when he was flying down the side of a mountain, he hit a bump and his leg flipped off. A ski with a boot and a leg hooked to it went speeding down the hill without Bill!

Standing below was a lady making her very first ski run. When she looked up she screamed, "Ski! Ski! No, leg! Leg!" Then her jaw dropped open when she saw Bill skiing down the mountain on one leg, chasing the other.

The runaway ski and leg stuck in the snow right in front of the lady. But Bill, nonplussed, brushed the snow from it, strapped it back on, and said, "It's okay, ma'am. Happens all the time."

Bill Latimer is a great man. He didn't stay down when he got knocked down. He didn't let obstacles and disappointments stop him. He overcame great emotional and physical barriers and succeeded.

Bill knows that you're never beat till you quit. One single event, even one as traumatic as an amputation, is merely a bump on the long ski run of life. With a sense of humor and a belief in self-competition, we can get up and do whatever it takes to succeed.

Be Above Average

Think for a moment about the effort it takes just to be average. Then consider how much energy Elaine Dart must put forth to be average. Born to a middle-class family, Elaine appears to be a typical girl with typical hobbies and interests. She paints a little, embroiders a little, knits sweaters, types on a computer, and does the basic things most average people do.

But Elaine has to work much harder. As a victim of cerebral palsy, she cannot use her arms. All the things you and I do with our hands, Elaine has to do with her feet. It took her two years to paint a picture, six months to embroider a pillow, and two years to knit a sweater. She can type a page in minutes, thread a needle in seconds, even write with a pen, all with her toes.

Consider the amount of effort Elaine must put forth just to be average and compare it with the individual effort you are making in your life. How do you stack up? Have you ever put that much effort into anything in your entire life? Imagine what you could do if you did.

Elaine Dart is a winner! She made the most of what she was given. For an average person, it doesn't take much effort to remain average. But the goal of every person should be to become something better. A winner is an average person who gives an above-average effort to make things happen.

Desire

Desire is an extraordinary, intense determination. It is a fighting heart with a burning commitment to a cause. This desire burns through in the field of athletic competition—where struggle is fierce and perseverance is profound. Sports competition is life personified.

To be successful in life, you must think like sports champions think: they believe they can run faster, jump higher, and throw farther than anyone else. That's why they continue to break world records. They understand desire, and they are willing to fight for it, regardless of the situation.

In 1975 during the U. S. Open Tennis Championships, a young tennis star from Spain named Manuel Orantes was struggling. No matter how hard he tried, the ball just didn't bounce well in his court. Nothing seemed to be going his way.

Being a great competitor, Manuel never gave up. He persevered one shot at a time through this long streak of bad luck. His toughness paid off. In the qualifying matches, Orantes was matched with the South American tennis star Guillermo Vilas.

As the match began, Manuel's confidence was restored. Certainly he could win. But contrary to his desire and belief, his string of misfortune continued. And before Orantes could even get focused, he found himself on the brink of being excluded from the tournament. It was the last point of the match. Vilas needed only one point to advance to the finals.

According to most experts, there was no believable way that Orantes could win. He was just too far behind. But did he believe this? No. Manuel Orantes is a champion; he is a winner and winners never give up.

Orantes started by winning the critical point and came back to win the semifinal match against Vilas. It was a grueling match, lasting more than five hours and ending at 1:30 in the morning. Orantes was worn-out physically, mentally, and emotionally, and it was theoretically impossible for him to win. But he did!

In the finals, luck should have been on his side of the court. But it wasn't. He was scheduled to play the top-ranked Jimmy Connors for the championship early the next day.

Because Orantes hadn't had much sleep, and because almost every ounce of energy had been drained from his body in winning against Vilas, the odds were against him. Somehow, Orantes found the strength to walk out onto the court and once again gave it his very best effort. As the underdog with everything going against him, including a low energy level, lack of sleep, blisters on the bottoms of his feet, and aching muscles, how could he possibly rise to the occasion?

His opponent, Jimmy Connors, was well rested and ready to go. It just didn't seem fair. But Manuel Orantes beat Jimmy Connors in straight sets 6–4, 6–3, 6–3. He fell to his knees after winning the last point and said a short prayer of thanks.

In an interview after the match, Orantes was asked how he did it. He replied, "When I walked out onto the court, I knew exactly what had to be done, and I knew that I didn't have the time or energy to dink around with Connors. If I was going to win, I was going to have to put him away as quickly as possible and beat him three sets to nothing. If I was going to win, it would be because of my desire."

What a great champion! He never gave up. He won because he believed that he could do it. It would have been easy for Orantes to concede defeat when he was so far behind Vilas, but he didn't. He wanted to win; therefore, he did win.

Remember, champions are average people like you and me. But they always give an above-average effort. That is their secret. Winners don't just dream and talk about winning—they do it!

After this loss and the lesson it taught him, the proud competitor, Jimmy Connors, developed his own never-say-never attitude. Since that turning point, he racked up more come-from-behind victories than any other tennis star in history. The name Jimmy Connors is still synonymous with desire, heart, and willingness to win.

Never Say Never

Richard Nelson, a sixteen-year-old junior at Manti High School in Utah, was an outstanding athlete. He was the number-two singles player on the state championship tennis team and had just made the basketball team that would go on that year to win the state championship. He was looking forward to much success as a senior during the following season. But on October 23, 1966, most of his athletic future was suddenly taken away from him.

That night, Richard was riding his bicycle from Manti to Gunnison to visit his girlfriend. The road was very steep in some places, which allowed Richard to reach speeds of forty miles per hour on the downhill slopes. Because it was dark and difficult to see, Richard was following the white line on the shoulder of the road to ensure his safety. As he came around a blind curve and was looking down at the ground, Richard failed to see a parked car jacked up to fix a flat tire on his side of the road. With no warning, he hit the parked car and ended up in the hospital, where he didn't regain consciousness for two days. Besides bad cuts on his head and knee, he broke his collarbone and right arm. He wore an L-shaped cast on his arm for two months. When the cast came off on December 29, Richard's doctor gave him a series of tests to determine the success of his healing. Richard failed all the tests. His triceps muscle had lost all its strength—he could not push out with his arm. The doctor diagnosed a pinched nerve and said that Richard might never regain the use of his right arm. Richard's once strong but now puny right arm just hung at his side, and the doctor gave him no real hope of recovery.

Because of his injury, Richard wasn't able to play on the basketball team during the rest of that year, but the coach made him equipment and statistics manager so that he could come to practice and be around the guys on the team.

His junior year ended, the summer came, and Richard was determined to do whatever he had to do to make the basketball team the next year. He realized that he couldn't make it right-handed, so he started working on his left-handed skills. All summer long, each and every night, he practiced making left-handed baskets at the outdoor courts in the center of town. Every night, he shot two hundred left-handed baskets and practiced left-handed dribbling and passing off the park retaining wall. Instead of going with his friends to the summer dances sponsored by the high school, Richard practiced basketball.

When the next season arrived, Richard was ready to try out for the team—and he made it! He never became a starter but he was always the first substitute to go in the game.

The season boiled down to the final game of the year against their archrival, Richfield High. This game would determine which team would win the league championship and advance to the state tournament playoffs. It was a "must win" for both teams.

On Friday night, the gym was packed. The starting guard for Manti had sprained his ankle earlier in the week, so Richard finally got his big break—he started the game! However, before the first quarter was over, Richard was replaced. It was hard to compete when he could only use one arm. The game continued until the last thirty seconds when Manti's other guard was injured, forcing Richard back into the game. Richfield was ahead by three points, and Manti had the ball. The Richfield team's coach tried to take advantage of the situation by having one of his players immediately foul Richard. Undaunted, Richard stepped up to the free throw line. (If he made the first foul shot, he would get a chance to shoot and make a second basket.) Confidently, Richard picked up the ball, braced it in his left hand, and shot. *Swish!* He made it, and the crowd went wild! He then made the next shot, bringing Manti High to within one point of Richfield. The crowd stood and went crazy again!

Richfield then took the ball out of bounds and threw a long pass down court to the player Richard was guarding, trying to make a quick, easy basket. But Richard, with his undying determination, leaped through the air to intercept the pass. When he landed he was fouled again, and was given another opportunity at the free throw line. With ten seconds left on the clock, Richard balanced the ball in his left hand, took a deep breath, and shot. The crowd was deathly quiet until— *swish*! He tied the game! His next shot went up, down and through. *Swish* again! He made it—he made all four shots—left-handed! Richard Nelson won the game and became the hero of the school.

According to Richard Nelson, he was not a hero. "Anybody could have done what I did," he said in his postgame interview. "I was supposed to make those shots. Everybody was counting on me to win the game when I was put in that situation. All I did was believe in myself, work hard when others didn't, and persevere. Anybody could have done what I did in the game if they had shot as many foul shots as I had shot last summer in practice." As Earl Nightingale said, "The only difference between a successful person and an unsuccessful person is that the successful person will do what the unsuccessful person will not do. The key is the successful person does not want to do it either, but then does it anyway."

It's Not Whether
You Win or Lose

A friend of mine experienced a miracle in a Mesa, Arizona, school that caters to learning disabled children. Randy Gray's young boy diligently does everything he can to learn and grow in strength. Every day, Randy stops by the school after work so the two of them can walk home together.

One afternoon, they walked past a park where some young men the boy knew were playing baseball. The boy asked, "Do you think they will let me play?"

His father knew that his son was not athletic, and because of his disabilities, most boys would not want him on their team. But his father understood that if his son was allowed to play, it would give him a much-needed sense of belonging.

The boy's father approached one of the young men and asked if his son could play. The boy looked around for guidance from his teammates. Getting none, he took matters into his own hands and said, "We're losing by six runs, and the game is in the eighth inning. I guess he can be on our team and we'll try to put him up to bat in the ninth inning." The father was ecstatic as his son smiled broadly.

In the bottom on the eighth inning, the losing team scored a few runs but was still behind by three. In the bottom of the ninth, the boy's team scored again, and now with two outs and the bases loaded, with the potential winning run on base, Randy's son was scheduled to be up to bat. Would the team actually let him bat at this juncture and give away their chance to win the game?

Surprisingly, the boy was given the bat. Everyone knew he was mentally and physically challenged. The boy didn't even know how to hold the bat properly, let alone hit. However, as he stepped up to the plate, the pitcher moved up a few steps to lob the ball in softly so he could at least make contact. The first pitch came in and the boy swung clumsily and missed. One of his teammates ran to him, and together they held the bat and faced the pitcher, waiting for the next throw. The pitcher again took a few steps forward to toss the ball softly toward the determined little boy. As the pitch came in, he and his teammate swung the bat, and together they hit a slow ground ball to the pitcher.

The pitcher picked up the soft grounder and could easily have thrown the ball to the first baseman. The little boy would have been out by a mile, and that would have ended the game. Instead, the pitcher took the ball and threw it on a high arc to right field, far beyond reach of the first baseman. Everyone started yelling, "Run, buddy, run to first. Run to first!" Never in his life had the boy run to first. He scampered and limped down the baseline wide-eyed and startled.

By the time he reached first base, the right fielder had the ball. He could have thrown the ball to the second baseman who would have tagged him out, but the right fielder understood what the pitcher's intentions were, so he threw the ball high and far over the third baseman's head. Everyone yelled, "Run to second, run to second." Again, startled, but with a grin on his face so big he could have eaten a banana sideways, the little guy ran. As he reached second base, the opposing shortstop ran to him, turned him in the direction of third base, and shouted, "Run to third." As he rounded third, the nine boys from each team ran behind him screaming, "Run, little buddy, run home!" He ran home and stepped on home plate. All eighteen boys from both teams lifted him on their shoulders and made him the hero. He had just hit a "grand slam" and won the game for his team!

With tears rolling down his face, Randy softly whispered, "I witnessed a real miracle that day. Not only did those eighteen boys realize the power of empathy, compassion, and service above self, but they let a father and his struggling son share together the power of a dream and the power of emotional connection that comes only through the magic of unconditional love!"

Rose

The first day of school, our professor introduced himself to our chemistry class and challenged us to get to know someone we did not know. I stood up to look around when a gentle hand touched my shoulder. I turned around to find a wrinkled older lady with a giant smile that lit up her entire face like a Christmas tree. She said, "Hi, handsome, my name is Rose. I am eighty-seven years old. Do you want to get lucky?"

I laughed and enthusiastically replied, "You incredible gorgeous babe, of course I do!" To which she gave me a mighty hug!

"Why are you in college at your young, innocent age?" I asked.

She kidded, "I'm here looking for a rich husband, you know, get married, have a couple of children, then retire and travel."

Hysterically laughing, I begged her to be serious. Her answer was simple but profound. "I always dreamed of having a college degree and so I'm getting one!"

After class, we walked to the student union building and shared a chocolate milkshake. It was obvious we were soul mates, and we became instant friends. In fact, every day for the next three months, we left class together, walked to the union building, and for at least an hour, I sat there in total awe listening to this "time machine" expound her wisdom and experience as she shared her life with me.

Over the course of the school year, Rose became a campus icon and generated attention everywhere she went. She loved to dress up and even occasionally wore miniskirts. Guys would whistle at her, and she would always respond by flashing a little leg. In the third week of school, she even got a tattoo that she loved to show off on her left shoulder. I teased her that I was hurt it didn't say "Dan." Of course, it was a magnificent rose.

At the end of the semester, we had Rose speak at our football banquet, and I'll never forget what she taught us. She was introduced and stepped to the podium. As she began to deliver her prepared speech, she dropped her 3 × 5 cards on the floor. Frustrated and a bit embarrassed, she leaned into the microphone and simply said, "I'm sorry I'm so jittery. I gave up beer for Lent and this whiskey is killing me! I'll never get my speech back together, so let me just tell you what I know." As we laughed, she cleared her throat and began.

"We do not stop playing because we are old. We grow old because we stop playing. There are only four secrets to staying young, being happy, and achieving success:

"(1) *Carpe diem* with humor. Seize each day with laughter.

"(2) You've got to have a dream. If you don't have a dream, how are you going to make a dream come true? When you lose your dreams, you die. That's why we have so many people walking around who are dead and they don't even know it!

"(3) There is a giant difference between growing older and growing up. If you are nineteen years old and lie in bed for one full year, and don't do one productive thing, you will turn twenty years old. If I am eighty-seven years old and stay in bed for a year, I will turn eighty-eight. Whoop-de-do! Anybody can grow older. That doesn't take any talent or ability. The idea is to grow up by always finding the opportunity in change.

"(4) Leave no regrets. The elderly usually don't have regrets for what we did, but rather for things we did not do. The only people who fear death are those with regrets."

At year's end, Rose finished her college degree she had begun all those years ago. One week after graduation, Rose died peacefully in her sleep. More than two thousand college students attended her funeral in tribute to the wonder woman who taught by example that it's never too late to be all you can possibly be!

The Last Game

It was the last football game of Brian's senior year, and a message came that his father had died. When the coach found out, he decided to tell Brian before the game, knowing he probably would elect not to play. But instead of reacting sorrowfully, Brian just took it all in stride and said, "I'll leave right after the game."

The coach had heard Brian speak highly of his father and expected him to grieve. When he didn't, the coach said, "Brian, you don't have to play. This game isn't that important."

Brian ignored him and played the game anyway. And play he did. Brian was the star, winning the game as a man possessed.

In the locker room, the other players showered with Brian. Some offered condolences, but most were appalled at his lack of sorrow. Brian was casual and happy, as if nothing had gone wrong. The coach was angry and worried that he had taught too much devotion to sports and not enough compassion. He scolded Brian, "Why did you play the game? Your father is dead. I'm ashamed of you and of myself."

Brian replied, "Coach, this was our last game. I am a senior. I had to play. This was the first time my dad has ever seen me play, and I had to play like I never played before."

The coach didn't understand.

With tears streaming down his cheeks, Brian replied, "You didn't know my father was blind, did you?"

Service

The Bellman

My dad battled cancer for six and a half years. He had a rare cancer called carcinoid that affected his intestines, stomach, and liver. As the pain mounted and Dad's last day approached, I decided I wanted to be by his bedside when he took his last breath. But that didn't happen. I was in Seattle, Washington, on two speaking engagements: a meeting on Friday morning and a convention on Saturday. I was staying at the Seattle Airport Marriott Hotel. It was early Friday morning, October 12. I had shaved and showered and put on my coat and tie when the phone rang. Thinking it was my ride to the convention, I picked up the phone and almost flippantly said, "I'll be right there." But instead, I just stood there. Fifteen seconds of silence later, my younger brother's voice pierced the quietness of the call. "Danny?"

Shocked, I tentatively answered, "Paul? What's up?"

Another fifteen seconds of silence started my heart pounding out of my chest. Then Paul confirmed my greatest fear. "Dad passed away this morning at seven." I sat down on the bed, and the tears immediately started to flow. I asked, "How is Mom?" He said, "Good." I said, "Give her a big hug and a kiss for me and tell her I'll phone her in a little while." Paul then asked me what I was going to do. After a moment of consideration I said, "I'm going to go make my speech. That's what Dad would want me to do. He always taught us to only make commitments that we can keep and to always keep those commitments." I thought it through out loud as I continued to talk to Paul, "I can't imagine what it would be like to be the meeting planner with more than twenty-five hundred people sitting in the audience, and not have the speaker show up. Dad always taught us to keep our promises. I need to stay here and speak and spend the night, speak tomorrow, and then hustle home. God knows I need your support, and hopefully I can give you some of mine. I know you and the rest of our family and Mom's huge circle of friends will comfort

Mom and each other. Mom will understand that my decision is exactly what Dad would want me to do. I'll talk to Mom later today and will see you tomorrow."

I hung up the phone and broke down, crying like a baby. My dad, my hero, was gone! And I was ripped and wrenched with the pain of regrets. Every thought and word was, "I wish, I shoulda, I woulda, I coulda, if only I had." For the record, I've done a lot of pretty cool things in my life (carried the Olympic Torch, flown in fighter jets, won a race-car driving school championship at Nürburgring in Germany, raced dogsleds, and slept in an igloo by the Arctic Sea). But I would trade it all for one more day with my dad! I miss him so much and have too many regrets!

As an author, I love to interview people—especially elderly people (elderly meaning someone older than me!). When I interview someone much older than me, the elderly person will always tell me they do not have regrets for things they did do; they only have regrets for things they did not do. Do you have regrets? Will you? I did. I still have regrets, and it's a living hell. Religion teaches that hell comes to the unbeliever after death. Yes, true. But I also believe that hell is where the man I am comes face-to-face with the man I could have been! I still have regrets with my dad, and I don't wish regrets on anyone.

Fifteen minutes had gone by when the phone rang again. This time it was my ride, and I told him I would be right down. I went into the washroom, splashed some water on my face to freshen up, left my room, and entered the elevator. As the elevator doors began to close, the corner of a bellman's cart crammed its way through the narrow opening, and the doors "binged" back open. Onto the elevator came an overzealous, way too cheery bellman. He pushed his cart to the middle, forcing me back to the rear corner. Trying to avoid eye contact, I stood with my head down, hands clasped in the "elevator position." As the doors closed, he blurted, "Yeehaw, Whoa-o-o! Did you see the beautiful sunshine today? I've lived here in Seattle all of my eighteen years, and it's rained every single day. You must have brought the good weather with you. How ya doin'?"

Not looking up, I said, "Fine." He kept staring at me until he again blurted, "No, sir, you're not fine. Your eyes are red and a little puffy. You've been crying." Instinctively I replied, "Yeah. I just found out my dad died this morning and I'm really sad." The bellman said, "Whoa," and went hauntingly quiet until the doors opened at the lobby. He went left, and I went right to the man waiting to give me a ride downtown to my meeting.

Fast-forward to the introduction of my speech. I had to dig deeper than I had ever dug in my life to rise to the occasion, but I did, and I made my speech. I know it's never appropriate to make yourself the hero of your own story, and I don't mean to. Making my dad proud of me for keeping my commitments and doing the right thing through service above self is the central point of this story.

At the end of my speech, I told the audience I would conclude with a song from one of my albums. I told them the reason I was singing it was that it was my dad's favorite song of all I had ever written, that he had died that morning, and therefore, it would be the first time he had ever heard me sing it in public. I finished the song and speech and had the driver take me to the Seattle Aquarium.

Why the aquarium? To run from change? To avoid pain? Absolutely not! Rather, to embrace every thought and emotion and realize four things: (1) In order to get a better answer, you must first ask a better question; (2) In life there are no mistakes, only lessons; (3) To go higher, you must first go deeper; and (4) Pain is a signal to grow, not to suffer. And once we learn the lesson the pain is teaching us, the pain goes away. That night at the aquarium, I "internally excavated" my innermost beliefs and feelings and remembered we're all going to die, so we have to deal with it by living every day to leave no regrets. Having learned the lessons, I had the driver take me back to the hotel.

I walked into the hotel room, and there on the chest of drawers was a basket of fruit. It wasn't your basic basket delivered from the hotel gift shop with the colored cellophane cover, ribbon bow, and small, sterile, stamped card from the manager that seldom gets your name right—"Thanks for staying with us, Ralphie." This basket was a broken basket, slightly smashed on one side. It appeared as if it was a last-minute gesture with no resources available. Whoever delivered it was obviously into presentation because the crinkled portion of the basket was turned toward the wall and covered by a big silky rubberized leaf that had apparently been picked off the fake tree in the lobby. In the basket were two oranges and an apple that had a little bite out of it. (Yes! No exaggeration!) Now, I don't think the deliverer got hungry on the way up to the room and snacked a bit. I believe he was into presentation and had found this huge, luscious, polished red apple that was perfect for his presentation. He couldn't help it if it had a crunch taken from it because the good definitely outweighed the bad and the color was important. The fruit basket also had in it a big ripe tomato and a long, thick carrot. Most important, in my basket was a handwritten note with several misspelled words that said, "Mr. Clark, I'm sure sorry your dad died. I was off work today at 5:00 PM, but I came back tonight so I could be here for you. Room service closes at 10:00 PM, but the kitchen has decided to stay open all night long so they can be here just for you. If you need anything, just call and ask for me. Signed, James—the bellman." James was not the only one to sign the card. Every single employee that night at the Seattle Airport Marriott Hotel signed my little card.

Let's put this experience into perspective and briefly rekindle the lesson learned. Here we have James, an eighteen-year-old young man, the youngest person on the entire employee payroll, who "gets it." Here we have James, the lowest-paid person on the entire employee payroll, who "gets it." "Gets" what? Service above self; internal stretch and change; behavior that exceeds external expectations; being more than we've been simply because we want to—motivated by the simple fact that we can!

He Who Travels the Road Best

Once upon a time, a king had a great highway built. Before he opened it to the public, he had a contest to see who could travel the highway best.

On the appointed day, the people came. Some had fine chariots; some used their feet. But no matter what vehicle they used, all of them complained that there was a large pile of rocks on the side of the road in one particular spot that hindered their progress.

At the end of the day, a lone traveler crossed the finish line and wearily walked over to the king. He was smudged with dirt, but he spoke with respect as he handed the monarch a bag of gold.

"I stopped along the way to clear a pile of rocks," he said. "And under it was a bag of gold. Can you find the rightful owner?"

Solemnly, the king replied, "You are the rightful owner. You have earned the gold by winning the contest. For he who travels the road best is he who makes the road smoother for those who follow."

So it is in life. While people scramble to outdo each other, every now and then a leader comes along to pave the way for the rest of us. To these leaders are given the rewards, the sacks of gold called gratitude, love, admiration, respect, and confirmation that their lives mattered.

Attention!

The occasion was the state high school conference for the Texans' War on Drugs. The setting was a high school gymnasium crammed with more than two thousand teenagers waiting for the opening general session to begin. A young man strolled up to the stage, stood on one foot with his left elbow resting on the podium, put his right hand on his stomach, and casually began to recite the Pledge of Allegiance. Suddenly a tall, dark-haired man rose from his chair on the stage. It was apparent that he was the director of the organization presiding over this event. The man walked to the podium and interrupted the young man's recitation.

"My name is General Robinson Risner. I was the highest-ranking prisoner of war in the Vietnam War. I spent seven years locked up in solitary confinement. I was tortured beyond belief. I limp because of it. Today I still have a hole in the front of my skull from the Chinese water torture inflicted on me. I willingly and proudly gave up years of my life defending our flag and our country and all the sacred and wonderful principles that they represent. America is the greatest country on the planet, the international leader of human rights, and of the free world. And you should show this country and her flag abiding respect. Hundreds of thousands of American soldiers have died for this flag. This young man's actions today are a disgrace to everything we hold dear—especially to the very freedom that allows us to gather here today. Therefore, let's do this again."

General Risner continued, "When we say the Pledge of Allegiance, we stand at attention. We place our right hands over our hearts, we look directly at the flag, and we say the words with conviction and pride. Please join me." A respectful silence filled the room. He then recited the Pledge in a way that I had never before heard—in a way that touched my life forever—in a way that taught everyone present the true meaning of *patriotism, duty, honor,* and *country.*

It's been a few years since that significant experience, yet every time I see an

American flag, I vividly remember it. The flag is more than colored cloth. It symbolizes everything for which America stands—every little thing and every single person that has ever contributed to making America great. Flag-burners and disrespectful leaders who flippantly mouth the words of our pledge should rethink their actions. You can be anti-war, anti-Democrat, anti-Republican, anti-guns, or anti-abortion—but don't ever be anti-American. The flag is not a symbol of any special interest group, political or social faction, racial group, or sexual preference. The flag is the symbol of a free republic and democratic society wherein we can all celebrate our differences, and more important, be free to do so. The flag is what binds us together.

The flag is part of you and it is part of me, and it waves for all the world to see everything we have the opportunity to be. Standing at attention for our flag is key. Show some dignity!

Free Enterprise

Because every person possesses the ability to get what he or she wants and to rise to the level of his or her own expectations, we need to become acquainted with an incentive system principle of success: free enterprise. The incentive system proves that there is no such thing as a financial crisis; it's only an idea crisis. Ideas create income. All we have to do is select what we want, find out how much it costs, and put together a step-by-step plan to make the necessary money. A few years ago, I had some dramatic opportunities to put this philosophy to the test.

Porsche (Project #1)—I had my eye on a charcoal gray Porsche for some time. Because of the high purchase price, I had to carefully budget my money so I could buy the sports car on the date that I chose—October 22.

For more than six months, I had been putting money aside so I could accomplish my goal. On October 12, ten days before the preset purchase date, I realized I was two thousand dollars short. How could I come up with that much money in a week and a half? Here was my chance to prove the financial crisis theory versus the idea crisis theory. Supposedly, all I needed was an idea, the right idea, and my financial crisis would be resolved.

I went to the local hardware store and explained my idea to the manager. He loved it and sold me 325 specially designed brass apparatuses at cost—$2.85 each. I purchased a drill bit that perfectly fit the diameter of the apparatuses, grabbed my electric drill, and headed into a neighborhood to try out my brilliant idea.

After an hour of practicing with my tools on an old piece of wood, I knocked on the first door. A lady and her husband answered. I said, "Ma'am, how do you know that I'm not a burglar?" Her husband immediately started to flex his neck and walked toward me with his fists clenched. I continued, "I'm not, so don't worry, but don't you think it would be a great idea if you could see who was on the other side of your door before you opened it?" The woman and her husband both agreed that it would be. Holding up some packages containing my invention, I said, "Good, because I'm selling these little peepholes, and I'd like to put one in your door!"

The man gave his okay and asked, "Could you put one in our back door, too?" On that Thursday, Friday, and Saturday, I installed more than three hundred peepholes, made a little more than twenty-one hundred dollars, and immediately went to buy my Porsche. Not bad, eh? The philosophy worked!

Paint (Project #2)—The next weekend, I had to prove to myself that my success hadn't been a fluke. I invested about ten dollars in some stencils, purchased some large cans of spray paint, and went into another neighborhood to test my idea. I don't know if your neighborhood has the tradition of painting your house numbers on the curb in front of your house, but this was my new service for sale. And if someone didn't have a curb, I sold him or her a big rock and painted the numbers on it. If they didn't want a rock, I painted the numbers on the mailbox. There was always a place to paint numbers; all I had to do was use my imagination. Several people I knew drove past in their cars and saw me sitting in the gutter painting. I could almost hear their conversations just by looking at their surprised faces. They seemed to be saying, "Oh look, Ethel. Dan Clark is in the gutter. Will he ever get a real job?"

I laughed to myself—all the way to the bank. Exactly one week from the day I bought my new car, I was completing a second Thursday, Friday, and Saturday sweep. I earned $1,942 painting numbers on curbs and rocks. It worked again and I purchased some exotic accessories for my Porsche.

Entrepreneur (Project #3)—Two weekends later, I was in San Antonio, Texas. I phoned one of my fun-loving friends to see how he was doing. It just so happened that he and his wife were planning to go to their local fair, so I tagged along for the company. Ted's wife attended some demonstration classes, so we decided we would do something to pass the time while we waited for her. I told Ted about my experiences with peepholes and painting, and he thought they were amusing. We started to brainstorm and laughed so hard thinking about the idea we had just had that we decided to go and pay the required fifty dollars to open up a booth at the fair. We found some supplies, made a sign, stapled it across the top of the booth, and started to package our product. I filled small plastic baggies and Ted drew labels. We sealed the baggies by folding the cardboard labels over the opening of the bag and stapling the sides of the folded labels together. What a professional job, they looked almost store-bought! And I'm sure our satisfied customers appreciated our first-class touch.

What did we successfully market? What was the gimmick that made people giggle and buy our product to show their friends? We put a few Cheerios in a baggie and cleverly sold them for $1.50 as "Doughnut Seeds"! By the end of the day, we had developed such a large clientele that we were forced to develop other product lines to accommodate the tastes of clients from other regions. The same Cheerios magically sold under a new name—"Bagel Seeds." Then we introduced little thistle burrs (the small parts of weeds that stick in our socks when we walk through a field). We bagged them and sold them as "Porcupine Eggs"! That day, Ted and I sold 457 baggies, splitting the gross income of $685.50 to net $300 each.

Yes, the free enterprise system, with its countless opportunities for entrepreneurship, works! But it only works when we do!

Land of Opportunity

Some people believe that America, as the "Land of Opportunity," is a thing of the past. They claim that it's too late in our history for anyone to start his or her own business, that every good idea has already been used. They claim it should easy to be successful. They want instant gratification, to which the products of the marketplace bear witness with their quick outcomes, from fast food to pain relief, to video games. When they find out that they have to pay their dues, that success takes time, education, hard work, and perseverance, they back off, clamoring for quotas and government subsidy. Everybody wants to succeed, but very few of us are willing to prepare to succeed.

Samuel Salter II was different. He didn't dwell on what he didn't have. He didn't harbor any feelings from the past history of his people and use those feelings as excuses to fail. Samuel saw obstacles not as stumbling blocks but as stepping-stones. He didn't dwell on his character deficits or on material things that he didn't have, but rather on the strength and assets he did have. He knew that God didn't make "junk" and didn't respect persons. Samuel knew God could bless him the same as anybody else. Samuel knew he had a bright mind, enthusiasm, and a desire to help others. He studied economics, opportunity cost, scarcity, and the fluctuating value of money. He even dabbled in real estate and began to offer his services to others. People were reluctant at first, but the word of his ability spread. Before Samuel knew it, he had an investment firm worth tens of thousands of dollars.

Amazingly, Samuel Salter II was only in high school when he began his firm. He was also an African American in an industry predominantly run by white men. We can all learn a valuable lesson from Samuel. Instead of waiting for the opportunity to knock, we should make things happen. Regardless of age, gender, race, or creed, America is still the Land of Opportunity. At the age of eighteen, Samuel was the youngest ever to receive the "Young Entrepreneur of the Year" award from

President Ronald Regan, and 20 years later, heads up an international sales, marketing finance company specializing in trade show marketing, generating leads, and on-line sales.

We see people from all walks of life succeeding in business, the arts, entertainment, and sports on a daily basis. Those who sit around whining "poor me" have nobody to blame but themselves. The doors to success are never locked. If they are closed, we need only turn the knob to open them and walk through. With enough preparation, education, and hard work, anybody in America can still get the job of his or her dreams instead of settling for second best. Remember that America's promise is not one of guaranteed security and success, but of life, liberty, and the opportunity to pursue happiness.

King for a Day

I have often been asked to speak on the topic of minority rights and cultural diversity. But instead of focusing on cultural diversity, and pointing out what makes us different, I always spend my time focusing on cultural commonality—what makes us the same. The same creator who made you made me too.

Equal opportunity is not the same as equal rights. If an important and mandatory meeting is being held upstairs on the second floor of a building, each of us has an equal right to attend. But if you are in a wheelchair and there is no elevator, you do not have an equal opportunity to attend, because it is not accessible to you.

When it comes to Human Rights, and celebrating our cultural commonality, we must acknowledge the fact that Availability is not the same as Accessibility. And in every one of our cultures, it is human nature to shun and turn away those who are different than us.

My friend and NBA Hall of Fame basketball superstar Kareem Abdul Jabbar experienced this firsthand after he graduated from the University of California at Los Angeles. In 1969, he was drafted into the NBA to play professional basketball and signed a lucrative contract. In his first year in the league, he was named Rookie of the Year!

When he returned to Los Angeles that summer and tried to rent an apartment in a nice part of town, Kareem was refused because he was black. Even though he was a celebrity, the landlord refused to rent him an apartment, just because he was a minority. They rented it to a white man two days later!

Five years later, when Kareem was traded to play for the Los Angeles Lakers, he purchased a home in the exclusive neighborhood of Bel Air. The original deed to the property stated that "No Negroes or Hispanics could hold title to the house."

Because of this social injustice, Kareem has always been a fan of Dr. Martin Luther King Jr., who in his own powerful way continually reminded us that when it comes to American human rights and civil liberties, we may have originally come to America on different ships, but we're all in the same boat now!

This is why we need to change and grow and update our understanding of what "different" really means. When we were young, educators tried to test our IQ by showing us a picture of three oranges and a pear. They asked us which one was different and did not belong, thereby teaching us that "different" equaled "wrong." They taught us to be conformists, with the stoicism of cows standing in the rain. What they should have taught us is that you don't get harmony when everybody sings the same note. Be *you*—you'll make a lousy somebody else!

Dr. Martin Luther King Jr. will always be revered as one of the greatest leaders of all time, regardless of race, country, or creed. He is a prime example of the beauty of democracy at work, a principle that Dr. King embraced in his soul. Armed with only his convictions, he set out, at the cost of his own life, to change an entire nation.

In the early days of the civil rights movement, his was the lone voice speaking out against the injustice of racial discrimination. He believed conflicts should be settled peacefully and legally, rather than violently. In the face of physical assault, Dr. King committed himself, and those around him, to nonviolent resistance. Who can ever forget the vicious dogs and fire hoses being set against the men, women, and children who were asking merely to be treated as human beings? Dr. King embodies the credo that all Americans should remember: We are created equal. To keep this ideal alive, we must all live by its philosophy every day.

From my perspective as a professional speaker committed to reaching people's emotions and positively affecting their lives by means of what my words evoke in them, Dr. King is a hero. Many orators have been as good, but none have been better. His powerful words still resonate in the hearts and souls of good, principle-centered people of every race:

> When evil men plot, good men must plan. When evil men burn and bomb, good men must build and bind. When evil men shout ugly words of hatred, good men commit themselves to the glories of love. Only through the bringing together of head and heart, intelligence and goodness, shall mankind rise to a fulfillment of his true nature. I have a dream that my four little children will one day live in a nation where they will not be judged by the color of their skin, but by the content of their character.

We miss you, Dr. King. The world is better simply because you passed through it. Oh, that we all could be "King for a day"!

He Gave It His All

Always in search of the next high adventure, I participated in a reenactment of the 1856 western migration of pioneers along the Oregon/Mormon Trail. From July 17–20, 2006, our group of 380 men, women, and teenagers picked up the historic trail on the plains of Wyoming at a place called Martin's Cove. It was here that the Martin Handcart Company sought shelter from a brutal storm in the fall of 1856. They had already pulled their five-hundred-pound handcarts from Omaha, Nebraska, and had worn out their shoes, some walking barefoot. Many wore torn, thin coats, and they had little food. Many died from exposure to the elements and were buried in shallow graves along the way.

With five to eight people assigned to each of our carts, our group left this special place pulling three-hundred-pound handcarts on a forty-one-mile, three-and-a-half-day trek that would take us up difficult soft-sand mountain climbs, back down dusty hills, twice across the Sweetwater River, and along flat plains in 100-degree weather—the hot sun always perched high overhead and the wind blowing dirt in our faces.

Our trek culminated in a five-and-a-half-mile climb over a steep, treacherous, extremely bumpy stretch of the historic Oregon/Mormon Trail called Rocky Ridge, appropriately named because of the countless sharp, jagged, sometimes large, and often-slippery rocks that poked out of the rutted ground. Completing this testy climb was rewarded by a fairly flat two-mile stretch that led to our final campsite. Rocky Ridge was one of the highest peaks on the more than thirteen hundred total miles of the trail and was just more than seven thousand feet elevation. Consequently, it took us four hours to pull and push our handcarts up and over the mountain and out to Rock Creek Camp.

As we concluded these seven and a half miles, we arrived at a small cemetery where thirteen gravestones honored those who had passed away at this location along the trail. It was here during an evening memorial service that I heard the following story. Having just experienced an unbelievable personal test of character that tested my will to succeed and my ability to endure to the end, I was moved to tears when I realized that what I had just accomplished was nothing compared to what the pioneers endured, experienced, and sacrificed in 1856—especially James Kirkwood. (The following account was taken from a journal entry of one who was there.)

James and his family came from Scotland. They had to save for a long time to be able to come to America. James's father got sick and died shortly after they arrived, but his mother was determined to fulfill her husband's dream and go on to the Salt Lake Valley. James was eleven years old and had three brothers: Thomas, nineteen, was crippled and had to ride in the handcart; Robert, twenty-one, helped their mother pull the cart. James was responsible for his younger brother, Joseph, who was four.

On October 20, 1856, the handcart company was camping by the Sweetwater River, not far from the base of Rocky Ridge. They had hardly had anything to eat for several days. Everyone was extremely weak, and there was two to three feet of snow on the ground. It was very cold, and ahead of them lay a long, steep climb through snow—sometimes as high as the axles on the handcarts. With freezing wind blowing in their faces and through their clothes, these pioneers traveled all day and all night.

Young Joseph's shoes had worn out from walking the previous thousand-plus miles, and his little feet were numb. Joseph fell down and started to cry. James tried to encourage him to climb some more, but Joseph couldn't take another step. That's when James picked him up and began to climb the ridge. Joseph was heavy, and James had to move slowly, carrying his little brother on his shoulder, then in his arms, then over his other shoulder. The two boys fell behind the main group, but James never gave up. Sometimes Joseph would start to slip because James's fingers were frozen, and he couldn't hold on very well. So he would set Joseph down and then immediately pick him up again and continue walking.

After taking more than twenty-seven hours to get up and over Rocky Ridge, James finally saw the fires burning at Rock Creek camp. The boys had made it to safety. James had been quiet for a long time, and young, thankful Joseph couldn't get him to talk. James gently dragged his little brother over to the rest of the group and carefully set him down by the fire. James then collapsed, never to get up again. Having given everything he had, eleven-year-old James Kirkwood lay down and died.

Because of stories like this, it behooves each of us to pause every once in a while to conduct a self-administered character audit and ask ourselves, *What am I made of? Would I have done this? Could I have done this?* In our day and age, the only ones who come close to understanding what it means to give it their all are our brave men and women who have served in the military and are currently fighting the global war on terrorism. Our fallen soldiers, airmen, sailors, and marines, like young James Kirkwood, made the ultimate sacrifice, unselfishly demonstrating, in the words of Jesus, that "greater love hath no man than this, that a man lay down his life for his friends."

Paying It Forward

It all began because my Dad didn't like Christmas—oh, not the true meaning of Christmas, but the commercial aspects of it, the overspending, the frantic running around at the last minute to get the gifts given in desperation because you couldn't think of anything else. Knowing he felt this way, my mother decided one year to bypass the usual material exchange. The inspiration came in an unusual way.

My younger brother, Paul, who was twelve that year, was playing in an All-star basketball tournament that hosted teams from all over the state. It lasted five days with a bracket format where each team played multiple games every day. By the end of the week a winner would be crowned.

Paul's first game was against a team sponsored by an inner-city church, whose roster was entirely made up of African American and Hispanic minority players. These youngsters, dressed in sneakers so ragged that shoestrings seemed to be the only thing holding them together, presented a sharp contrast to our boys in their cool red and white uniforms and flashy new shoes. We ended up walloping them. And because Paul's games were all played on the same court as this inner-city team, over the course of the day we ended up staying and watching every team beat them.

The motivating thing to me was that even though they kept losing, they never seemed to get down. In fact, while waiting for their next game to start, they actually swaggered around with a kind of proud street pride that couldn't acknowledge defeat.

Dad, seated between Mom and me, shook his head sadly. "I wish they could win at least one game," he said. "They have a lot of potential, but if they keep losing like this it will take the heart right out of them." Dad loved kids, all kids, especially the underserved. That's when the idea for his present came. That afternoon, Mom went to a local sporting goods store and bought twelve pairs of basketball shoes with an agreement with the store manager that the young men could exchange them for the right size and color of their choosing. Mom then delivered them anonymously to the inner-city church. On Christmas Eve, she placed an envelope on the tree, the note inside telling Dad what she had done and that this was his gift from her.

His smile was the brightest thing about Christmas that year and in succeeding years. For each Christmas, Mom followed the tradition—one year sending a group of Polynesian kids to a football game, another year a check to a group home for troubled teens so Santa could come.

The envelope became the highlight of our Christmas. It was always the last thing opened on Christmas morning, and my siblings and I, ignoring our new toys, would stand with wide-eyed anticipation as Dad lifted the envelope from the tree to reveal its contents. As we children grew, the toys gave way to more practical presents, but the envelope never lost its allure. The story doesn't end there.

You see, we lost Dad to cancer in October. When Christmas rolled around, Mom was still so wrapped up in grief that she barely got the tree up. But Christmas Eve found her placing an envelope on the tree, and in the morning, it was joined by four more. Each of us children, unbeknownst to the others, had placed an envelope on the tree for our Dad. The tradition has been perpetuated in my family and as we continue to Pay it Forward, it will one day expand even further, with our grandchildren standing around the tree, in wide-eyed anticipation, watching as their fathers take down the envelope. Dad's spirit, like the Christmas spirit, will always be with us.

Operation Smile

When Dr. Bill Magee graduated from medical school, he and his wife Kathy, a nurse, decided to volunteer their time and talents and organize some other doctors to travel to the Philippines on a humanitarian medical mission. Dr. Magee's specialty was plastic surgery, and the intent of the mission was to correct facial deformities and repair the cleft lips and cleft palates of the poor and underserved children of that country. With limited time, supplies, and resources, the doctors did all they could, but had to turn away hundreds of heartbroken mothers and crying children.

Realizing the incalculable need for their services, Dr. Magee and his wife Kathy made a commitment to return. Operation Smile was conceived and born that day.

Word spread throughout the land, and the anticipation of the returning doctors excited those who needed their help. One man, twenty-three-year-old José, heard about these amazing surgeries, and although he lived in a village three and a half-days journey away, he felt this was his hope for relief and set out for Manila.

José had a three-pound tumor growing from his chin that was so large and grotesque that his family kept him hidden from public view his entire life. His religious culture believed he had this facial deformity because he was possessed by the devil, he was never allowed to attend school, no one would hire him to work, and if and when he ever did go outside, it was at night and he always wore a bandana to hide his tumor.

José had lived for twenty-three years as a prisoner in his own body, and word that doctors were coming to perform free surgeries ignited in him a spark of hope he had never had.

With no money for travel, José secured his bandana over his face and set out on his long three and a half day journey. It was literally like Planes, Trains & Automobiles as he walked over a rugged mountain pass, forged through a river, and trekked for countless miles along the dusty back roads of the Philippines until he finally arrived in Manila. Amidst hundreds of mothers and fathers and their small children, he was the lone adult hoping for a miracle, sleeping on the ground outside the hospital facility waiting for the morning to come.

As the screening process got under way, and the criterion for care was established, José did not qualify for treatment because he did not have a cleft lip or pallet condition, and the priority of the mission was pediatric care. Because there were so many children that required surgery, José was turned away. Sadly, he walked the three and a half-day journey back home to his village.

Six months later, the word spread that Operation Smile was returning to Manila. Thinking he would give it another chance, José again made the three and a half-day journey only to be turned away a second time for the same reasons. Devastated, he walked back home.

Six months later, José heard Operation Smile was returning to Manila, and on the verge of suicide believing his life didn't matter to anyone, he decided to try his luck one last time. He sold his goat, which was his only possession, to get enough money to travel by bus and boat, and, in turn, showed up on time at the screening.

This time José's name was posted on the board, and his name was the last one called. He had passed the screening tests and would receive his surgery the next morning! As José was given his number, he turned to proceed to the processing area with never before experienced excitement. He started thinking about all the ways his life would immediately change. He had never kissed his mother good night. Maybe he could actually and finally have a friend?

Suddenly, José noticed a devastated, crying mother whose little girl would have been next in line for surgery except for the lack of resources. He quickly rationalized that he was old, and so this little girl would never have to go through life in the lonely, ridiculed way he had, he gave his number to the mother! With tears in his eyes, not knowing if he would ever have this chance again, José turned and slowly trekked his way home, uncertain if he wanted to live one more day.

When Dr. McGee found out about this experience, he immediately cross referenced the medical information they had acquired during the screening and tracked down José in his village. With the help of some donors, they arranged for José to be flown by helicopter to Manila and then on to Norfolk Virginia, where Dr. McGee and a team of extraordinarily skilled surgeons performed a series of nine surgeries over the course of several weeks to remove the three-pound tumor.

I first met José when we shared the program as keynote speakers at an International Operation Smile Youth Leadership Conference. After I heard this story, I was deeply and emotionally touched when the handsome, smiling, confident, articulate José finished his speech by singing a song he had written about Operation Smile as we all gazed at the huge photograph of him in a white tuxedo standing next to his beautiful wife, holding their beautiful newborn baby!

This is what Operation Smile is all about— changing the world one person, one smile, one family, one village, one country at a time!

Locked Doors

Everybody has heard of Harry Houdini, the master magician and escape artist. He often boasted that he could escape from any jail in the world in less than an hour, if he was allowed to wear street clothes.

A small town in the British Isles took Houdini up on his challenge. When Houdini arrived at the town's new jail, excitement was at a fever pitch as he was taken to the cell. Confidence oozed from every pore as the door was closed.

Hidden in his belt was a ten-inch piece of steel that he used to work the lock. At the end of thirty minutes, his confident look had disappeared. At the end of an hour, he was drenched in perspiration. After two hours, he literally collapsed against the door. And, amazingly, the door opened.

It had never been locked, except in Harry Houdini's head. One little push would have opened it. But since he thought it was locked, he didn't try.

The doors of opportunity are the same. If we think they are locked, we won't try to open them. But sometimes, all it takes for them to swing wideopen is one extra push.

Are you trying everything you can to open the doors of opportunity in your own personal world? Maybe some of the doors you didn't think you could open are waiting for you to use them. Try believing the door is open before you give up.

Saved by the Book

One day, when I was a freshman in high school, I saw a kid from my class walking home from school. His name was Kyle. It looked like he was carrying all of his books. I thought to myself, *Why would anyone bring home all his books on a Friday? He must really be a nerd.* I had quite a weekend planned (parties and a football game with my friends Saturday afternoon), so I shrugged my shoulders and went on. As I was walking, I saw a bunch of kids running toward him. They ran at him, knocking all his books out of his arms and tripping him so he landed in the dirt. His glasses went flying, and I saw them land in the grass about ten feet from him. He looked up and I saw this terrible sadness in his eyes.

My heart went out to him. So, I jogged over to him. As he crawled around looking for his glasses, a tear fell from his eye. I handed him his glasses and said, "Those guys are jerks. They really should get lives." He looked at me and said, "Hey, thanks!" There was a big smile on his face. It was one of those smiles that showed real gratitude. I helped him pick up his books and asked him where he lived. As it turned out, he lived near me, so I asked him why I had never seen him before. He said he had gone to private school before now. I would have never hung out with a private school kid before. We talked all the way home, and I carried his books. He turned out to be a pretty cool kid. I asked him if he wanted to play football on Saturday with me and my friends. He said yes. We hung all weekend, and the more I got to know Kyle, the more I liked him. And my friends thought the same of him.

Monday morning came, and there was Kyle with the huge stack of books again. I stopped him and said, "Boy, you are gonna really build some serious muscles with this pile of books every day!" He just laughed and handed me half the books. Over the next four years, Kyle and I became best friends. When we were seniors and began to think about college, Kyle decided on Georgetown. I was going to

Duke. I knew that we would always be friends, and that the miles would never be a problem. He was going to be a doctor, and I was going for business on a football scholarship.

Kyle was valedictorian of our class. I teased him all the time about being a nerd. He had to prepare a speech for graduation. I was so glad it wasn't me having to get up there and speak. On graduation day, Kyle looked great. He was one of those guys that really found himself during high school. He filled out and actually looked good in glasses. He had more dates than I did, and all the girls loved him! Boy, sometimes I was jealous. Today was one of those days. I could see that he was nervous about his speech. So I smacked him on the back and said, "Hey, big guy, you'll be great!" He looked at me with one of those looks (the really grateful one) and smiled. "Thanks," he said.

As he started his speech, he cleared his throat and began. "Graduation is a time to thank those who helped you make it through those tough years. Your parents, your teachers, your siblings, maybe a coach . . . but mostly your friends. I am here to tell all of you that being a friend to someone is the best gift you can give them. I am going to tell you a story." With disbelief, I sat mesmerized as he told the story of the first day we met.

He had planned to kill himself over the weekend. He talked of how he had cleaned out his locker so his mom wouldn't have to do it later and was carrying all of his books and the rest of his stuff home. He looked hard at me and gave me a little smile. "Thankfully, I was saved. My friend saved me from doing the unspeakable." I heard the gasp go through the crowd as this handsome, popular boy told us all about his weakest moment. I saw his mom and dad looking at me and smiling that same grateful smile. Not until that moment did I realize its depth.

Never underestimate the power of your actions. With one small gesture, you can change a person's life.

From Slums to Judge

Joseph Sorrentino, a juvenile court judge from Los Angeles, proves that life is a story.

He was born and raised in Brooklyn. He was the second-eldest in a family of seven children, and he grew up in an atmosphere of street gangs and hoodlums. By the time he was twenty years old, Joe had served time in reform school, jail, the brig, and even a padded cell. He flunked out of school four times, went through nearly thirty jobs, and was kicked out of the Marine Corps.

As a high school dropout with no skills and no money, he tried his hand at professional boxing. He soon quit that as well.

One day, as he was passing Brooklyn's Erasmus Hall High School, Joe saw a sign that invited passersby to enroll in night school. Suddenly, he realized that his only chance for a better life was through education, and his inadequacies hit him like a ton of bricks.

Joe enrolled, found that he loved to learn, and graduated with the highest grade point average in the history of Erasmus Hall's night school. He then decided to attend the University of California at Santa Barbara, where he became president of the student body and graduated magna cum laude. After graduation, he began reviewing his life with all its defeats and decided there was one more thing he should do before he tackled the real world. He reenlisted in the Marines to remove that embarrassing blemish from his record. After an honorable discharge, he entered Harvard Law School and graduated as class valedictorian in 1967.

His valedictory address touched everyone present, as he recounted his life story and concluded with these words: "Do not look for tragedy or trauma to explain the change in me; it came mainly from inner resolution. Life is a story, and as the author of my own never-before-written story, I had the right and the chance to write it and rewrite it so that it would play out in whatever way I desired."

Why Should I?

Have you ever volunteered for something? Why did you do it? How did you feel when you finished?

Volunteers arrive early, stay late, go without breaks, and always smile. Why? They are not paid, yet they give their all. Can you imagine what would happen to the work ethic of our workforce if everybody approached his or her job in the volunteer spirit of "I want to" rather than in the contractual agreement spirit of "I have to"? Contracts bind performance and breed minimum required involvement. Volunteerism also binds performance, while simultaneously breeding maximum productivity.

Imagine what America would be like without volunteers. Consider the organizations that depend on volunteers: churches, youth groups, healthcare agencies, hospitals, schools, civic organizations, sports leagues, arts and humanitarian associations, environmental groups—in every community throughout this country. Our quality of life would be infinitely less rewarding if it were not for the volunteers who selflessly offer their time while receiving no pay—and often little or no recognition.

What is the force behind these remarkable efforts and great desire to help others? Volunteers find the work extremely satisfying and fulfilling. Volunteering builds self-esteem and develops personal skills. It teaches us how to use our time more productively. More important, it teaches us that it isn't always what you have, but more often what you give away that matters most in life. It teaches us to place a greater value on what we contribute to society than on what we accumulate.

Our sense of community is the strongest tradition in the history of American values, and it's the volunteers who provide this strength. Through volunteering, we make more than just a living with our lives—we make a difference and create "ordinary" miracles. May each of us volunteer to make and keep America the greatest, freest, bravest, friendliest, cleanest, kindest, most peaceful, most helpful, and most courteous country in the world!

Love

Law of Attraction

We become the average of the five people we associate with the most. There-fore, we must be willing to pay any price and travel any distance to associate with extraordinary human beings. What you think about and believe in is what you attract; when you attract those new thoughts and ideas, you begin to assimilate them into who you are. If your desire is to attract positive people and positive opportunities, you must be a positive person creating positive opportunities. The Law of Attraction is no secret. It's been around for thousands of years and is simi-lar to the Law of the Harvest in that we reap only what sow – input equals output 100 percent of the time.

The fundamental governing principle of the Law of Attraction is: Likes Attract Likes. You are a magnet, attracting everything to you, and this unfathomable mag-netic power is emitted through your thoughts.

A very well-known and well documented example of the Law of Attraction is the placebo effect, most of which occur in medication trials. Patients who believed they would be affected positively by the medications fared better than those who did not, even when given an inert tablet (often a sugar pill).

Every one of us puts out a measurable energy that falls into a specific frequency that can only be felt by someone on that same frequency. Are you putting out posi-tive or negative energy? Look around. Are you attractive or unattractive? If you don't like your current program and the vibe you're obviously dialed in to, finely-tune who you are, tune in to your true frequency, and start sending that energy out! One wavelength, one frequency, one signal and one vibe can only attract the same wavelength, and same frequency, signal and vibe. "Likes Attract Likes" is a principle of the universe that never changes for anyone or anything.

The next time you're driving down the winding road of life tuned into your program of choice, and for some reason you lose your connection, instead of continuing on and frantically changing your channel to settle for a sub-par shallow, temporary program fix that is easily found and commonly heard, why not stop, eliminate the distractions that are blocking your reception, and go where you can hear and feel, fully experience and easily tune back in to the frequency and deeper, meaningful program that you enjoyed before. It is there. The program is always broadcasting. But it is our responsibility to find it and tune into it!

When it comes to the Law of Attraction we must never think it's a "build it and they will come" proposition. Obeying the Law of Attraction means we are always bettering ourselves to be more interesting and appealing, and actively searching for the individuals who share this same passion, purpose and desire to connect with us. When our energy guides us to each other, and our frequencies perfectly match up, and our communication vibes are strong, and the signals are coming in loud and clear, it is beautiful at home, at work, at play, on a team, in a business deal, in a military squadron or platoon, in community service, and especially in the arms of our "one and only"! Regardless if it's a personal or professional relationship, our feelings are a feedback mechanism to us about whether we are on track or not, whether we're on course or off course.

Of all the questions you may have, the most important to be clear about are "What do I want? What is possible to achieve? Do I actually believe I can get it—with my weaknesses and limitations and my strengths? And, do I believe I deserve it?" Honestly answering these inquiries is fundamental in creating and projecting our chosen energy force, wavelength frequency, and continual energy flow. To illustrate, let's talk about the process of purchasing an automobile.

The first question: do you deserve to drive a new car or a used car? Whatever you choice, you immediately notice others driving similar conditioned cars. In my case, a few years ago I decided I deserved to buy me my dream sports car. I was in Hawaii and paid good money to rent a red Ferrari. What a joke! I removed the coupe hard top to make it a convertible, and the windshield came up to my chin. My head stuck out the top and I looked like Mr. Potato Head! I had to duck to drive and couldn't even get it out of first gear!

After much searching I finally discovered the Porsche had plenty of headroom and I decided that I deserved to own and drive one. And what happened when I got "clear" on what kind of a new car I was going to buy? I suddenly started noticing how many cars were like mine on the streets and highways. A guy at the end of my street drives a Porsche and until I knew what I wanted, I had not noticed his car before. Then I got clear on the style I wanted and focused my energies on buy-ing a 911 GT3, fuel injected and turbo-charged with a whale-fin on the back. And do you know what happened? I was blown away by how many 911 GT3 Porsches with a whale-fin on the back there were in my community. Then I got even clearer and decided it should be charcoal grey.

And what happened? Although there weren't a lot of them on the road, it was amazing how we seemed to find each other. In one week I saw five other cars exactly like mine. In fact, one night I pulled into the left hand turn lane at an intersection and a Porsche that looked exactly like mine pulled into the left lane across from me. It was instant brotherhood. He flashed his headlights, so I flashed mine back. He flashed them again and I flashed back! We flashed hand fist pumps and exchanged smiles to acknowledge what we had in common and then drove away. Isn't it interesting that this Law of Attraction also holds true when it comes to belief? When you have become clear on what you believe, it is obvious that you automatically attract others who believe as you believe. Positive attracts positive – miserable being finds other miserable being, and then they are happy!

The same thing holds true for someone who thinks they only deserve to drive a used car. They pull into the left hand turn lane at an intersection in their rusted out 1977 Buick with a broken muffler, a bad air shock and two toned paint chipping away, and sure enough, another 1977 beat up Buick pulls into the left hand turn lane facing them. Just like with a new car, it is still instantaneous brotherhood as the guy flashes you his one headlight, you flash your one headlight back, and together smile with that look, "Yo Dude, whats up? Yea –a food stamps, welfare, represent homie!"

Obviously this analogy has nothing to do with socio-economic conditions. When you put a hard-to-catch horse in the same field as an easy-to-catch horse, you usually end up with two hard-to-catch horses. When you put a sick child in the same room with a healthy child, you usually end up with two sick children. To be disciplined, healthy and great we must associate with the disciplined, healthy and great ones. I see wonderful women doing everything they know how to do to get out of a physically and emotionally abusive relationship, only to jump back into a more dysfunctional relationship with a bigger loser than the bum she just kicked out. Why? Likes attract likes. The primary goal in life should not be to get what we think we want, but to want what we get. If you don't like what you attracting, change what's attracting it.

Be Not Weary

Sally thought she saw life change for the better when a widower from her past returned with a proposal of marriage. Nicely attired, he spoke of a prosperous farm. Sally understood him to mention servants, and that meant that he must be a man of substance. She accepted his offer and crossed the river with him to view her new possessions, only to find a farm surrounded by wild blackberry vines. The house was a floorless, windowless hut. The imaginary servants were two thinly clad, barefoot children. She soon discovered that the father had borrowed the suit and boots to go a'courting. Her first thought was to go back home.

But she looked at the youngest boy, whose gaze met hers, and she decided to stay for the sake of the children who needed a mother.

Each of us has been in her position, wanting to leave the place we find ourselves in. It's always easier to let somebody else take responsibility for a seemingly hopeless situation.

But never despair. A boy is the only thing God has out of which to make a man. Sometimes all he needs is a teacher.

Sally Bush didn't know when she looked at the melancholic ten-year-old face that her new stepson's name was Abraham Lincoln.

The Miracle of Casey

Little Casey was five years old when I met her. She was one of the most beautiful, bubbly little girls in the entire world. She was diagnosed with leukemia and was scheduled for a bone-marrow transplant at Doernbecher Children's Hospital in Portland, Oregon. After the frightening, tedious surgery, Casey would need to stay in Portland for months of chemotherapy and radiation treatment. Her mother, Pam, wanted to stay by her side the entire time, but it was impossible financially.

Pam was a schoolteacher in Albany, Oregon, and couldn't afford time off from work. She prayed and pleaded for a miracle.

The miracle of precious little Casey started in the hospital with the capable doctors and nurses who treated and cared for her. The miracle extended when Pam was welcomed to stay at the fabulous Ronald McDonald House in Portland—at no charge.

The medical bills were insurmountably high. In Pam's greatest moment of despair, her fellow teachers at South Albany High School helped by creating a daily class schedule where each teacher coordinated his or her personal and professional schedules to cover Pam's classes. This allowed them to fulfill her obligations without paying for a substitute teacher, and while Pam moved to Portland to be by Casey's side, she didn't miss a single paycheck.

Casey brought help, joy, love, and dreams to everyone who had the privilege of being around her. She was in remission and on her way to recovering, so her sudden death shocked and saddened all of us. She passed away on Good Friday 1994, at ten years of age.

We pray for miracles, but God answers our prayers and fulfills our needs through other people. Sometimes we don't get the answers we choose, and we often don't understand the answers we get. But one thing is for sure. If God had come to Casey's mother and said, "Pam, you can either have Casey for ten years or not at all, which do you choose?" I guarantee Pam would have said, "Give me sweet Casey for ten years."

In her short life, Casey Weiler brought a hospital staff together, a high school faculty together, and my own mind, heart, spirit, and soul together in focus. Thanks, Casey, for teaching us about unselfish service, unbridled hope and optimism, enduring to the end with a smile, and a clear understanding of what really matters most.

Forgive the Mistakes of Others

Paul was nervous as he sat on the train; the old man sitting next to him sensed this.

"Son, what's the matter with you?"

"I just got out of prison," replied Paul. "My mistake broke my parents' hearts and caused them a lot of shame. I don't know if they can love me after what I did. I never let them visit me in prison. I told them they didn't have to let me come home if they were too ashamed of me. I live in a small town with a large tree by the railroad tracks. I told them to tie a ribbon around that old tree if they were willing to let me get off."

Paul paused as the old man listened, then continued.

"The reason I'm so nervous is that we're almost there and I'm scared to look at that tree. I feel I don't deserve my parents' forgiveness because I hurt them so much."

Paul looked down in shame. Neither man spoke as the train slowed down to stop at the next station, Paul's hometown. Then the old man nudged him, "I think you can look now, son."

Paul glanced up slowly. The old tree was covered with ribbons—red, blue, yellow, orange, and green—hundreds of them. Paul turned to the old man with tears in his eyes and said, "They still love me. I'm going home."

Whether you first heard a story like this in a well-known song or are hearing it for the first time, it's a great example of unconditional, nonjudgmental love. If you aren't getting along with someone in your family because of something they've done, maybe it's time to let them know you still care. Tell them how you feel!

What Really Makes a Leader?

During the 1968 Special Olympics, a special competition for mentally and physically challenged athletes, Kim Peek was competing in the fifty-yard dash.

Kim had brain damage and was physically challenged. He was racing against two other cerebral palsy victims. They were in wheelchairs and Kim was the lone runner. As the gun sounded, Kim moved quickly ahead. Ten yards from the finish line, he turned to see how the others were doing. One girl had turned her wheelchair around and was stuck against the wall. The other boy was pushing his wheelchair with his feet.

Kim stopped and retraced his steps. He pushed the little girl across the finish line. Meanwhile, the boy going backward won the race. The girl took second and Kim lost.

Or did he?

The greatest leader and champion doesn't always win the race but gains honor and recognition by serving others.

Pass It On

The scene was a national convention of a well-known Fortune 500 company. The speaker at the opening general session interrupted his presentation to interact with the audience and make a significant point. He asked everyone to stand up, team-up two by two, and face each other. "With all sincerity," he said, "and with a straight face, tell that person 'I love you' and then give them a hug." Everybody laughed and proceeded with caution. Man-to-man laughed and turned sideways to slap each other on the back inside shoulder-to-inside shoulder. Woman-to-woman laughed and actually hugged face-to-face. Woman-to-man was different. With bodies poking way out and one shoulder leaning way in, they awkwardly stood at arm's length and quickly patted each other on the back as if they were burping a baby.

The speaker's point was to get people to think and step outside their comfort zones. Through this simple exercise, it became obvious to everyone that we change only when it's safe, only when it's required, and, most likely, only for that moment.

When the speaker finished, the president/CEO stood up to thank him. "The speaker was great and said some magnificent things, but the most powerful thing he did was invite us to break the old-mold expectation that work relationships must be all business, cognitive, standoffish, and nonemotional. When he invited us to say 'I love you' to a business associate, it hit me hard that this is one of the major ingredients missing in our organization. From this day forward, our corporate culture will stress emotional human connection. I trust each of you will continue to use good judgment and remain first-class in your treatment to one another, but please, I repeat, please, freely express your appreciation to one another. And when given permission, don't be afraid to 'appropriately hug.' You never know, this thanking, needing stuff could be contagious. Pass it on!"

The CEO left the meeting, got into his chauffeur-driven town car, and headed home. As he thanked his driver for opening his door, he leaned over and briefly hugged him. "Thanks," the CEO said. "For four years, you have been my company driver, and I don't think I have ever told you how wonderful you are. You are the best driver on the road. You are a first-class gentleman and an asset to our organization. I need you and deeply appreciate your friendship and loyalty."

The chauffeur walked through the front door of his home, whistling and smiling like never before. He picked his wife up off the floor and hugged her close. "I changed my mind. I'm not going to quit my job after all."

"Why?" she asked. "Did you get a raise or something?"

"Yes I did. You know my boss pays me way more than other drivers, and I make a great living. I wasn't looking for more money. Today Mr. Allen gave me an emotional raise—the raise I've been seeking and needing for more than a year! Get ready, I'm taking you to dinner."

They went to a restaurant they had never been to before. Their son worked there. His father had kicked him out of the house a year ago. When the son saw them walk in, he tried to hide, but couldn't. His purple Mohawk hair stood up, and the ring and chain in his nose hinged off his dog-collar necklace. The son didn't know what to say or do, but his father did. He walked straight over to his son and hugged him. With tears in his eyes he said, "I love you, son. I appreciate you for you. Please come home. I miss you and need a relationship with you."

The startled boy nervously hugged him back and excused himself to go into the kitchen. "I've decided not to quit this job and move to San Francisco," he told his manager. "I've just decided to move back in with my parents. I'm going back to school to get my GED."

"Why?" the manager asked.

"I just discovered my parents actually care about me and I'm sick of letting them down trying to prove my independence. It's time to make them proud!"

Great story, but let's take it further. This son's eventual children will now benefit from his education, higher expectations, inner peace, and stability. They will most likely experience his unconditional love, hugs, and appreciation. As he and his wife pass it on, their children's children will be the recipients of their hugs and appreciation. As they pass it on, their children's children will be. . . .

A Mother's Example

There were four clergymen who were discussing the merits of the various translations of the Bible. One liked the King James Version best because of its simple, beautiful English.

Another liked the American Revised Version best because it is more literal and comes nearer to the original Hebrew and Greek.

Still, another liked Moffat's translation because of its up-to-date vocabulary.

The fourth minister was silent. When asked to express his opinion, he replied, "I like my mother's translation best."

The other three expressed surprise. They did not know that his mother had translated the Bible.

But he assured them, "She translated it into life, every day of her life, and it was the most convincing translation I ever saw."

The Worth of a Soul

It was Friday, the last day of the semester, the last day of Christy's university experience. She was finally done. She would get her degree!

It started out as a cold, miserable day. Christy had just taken a final exam in statistics and was walking across campus to get into her car to drive to her apartment to begin her well-deserved and meticulously planned-out, party-packed weekend. Two days of late-night cramming, an overabundance of caffeine in her system, and stress from the fact she had forgotten the obvious answers to three of the easiest questions on the test had left Christy a bona fide mess. She was tired, her back hurt, she had recently developed blisters on her foot from her new hiking boots, and in her mind, she had every excuse not to be at school.

As the wind and lashing rain picked up, so did Christy's effort to get home. She started to jog. When she arrived at the last intersection across the street from the student parking lot, Christy met up with a fellow student. She didn't know him and had never said hello, but she had seen him several times driving around campus in his wheelchair.

The light finally changed, and Christy started to walk. Halfway across the street, she heard a sound of desperation. Christy stopped, went back to the man, and stooped down in an attempt to hear him more clearly through the whistling storm. He pointed down at his tires and forced out the word "stuck." His wheelchair was caught on a small rock. With each effort to free himself, his wheels spun a deeper rut in the mud. It turned out this man had a form of cerebral palsy that affected his speech. His muscles and motor skills were deficient in his legs, and his hands were gnarled and contorted. Somehow, though, he was a self-sufficient student at the university who managed to get himself around in his manually propelled wheelchair.

Christy freed his wheelchair and pushed him over the rocks, through the muck, and over to the other side of the street. He said something else she did not understand but concluded with a distinct "Thonk you" as they parted ways. Christy went left into the parking lot, and he turned right to continue up the road.

As Christy escaped the horrible weather and slid into her comfortable car, she started it up with the warm heater blowing and wiped her hair and face with a towel she had on the seat. Out of breath and chilled to the bone, Christy couldn't help but look out her window and notice the man struggling to propel his wheelchair against the fierce wind blowing directly in his face. One push at a time, he inched his way up the hill.

Anyone with a conscience would have helped him, and Christy broke down. She knew she was in a hurry to meet her friends at their favorite watering hole, but she had to follow her heart. Christy turned off the car and reluctantly walked to meet him. As she battled the freezing rain, the only motivating thought that kept her going was the presumed short distance and short time involved. Surely he lived in the next block, and she would push him to his apartment and then run back to her warm car.

Christy touched his shoulder, and it startled him into a shocked gasp that quickly turned into a warm, smiling face with grateful eyes and a struggling outstretched hand of fellowship. "Hel—lo," he slowly greeted. "Ma na—me Jordan."

Christy answered, "Hi, Jordan," and told him she wanted to push him to his home if he would tell her where he lived.

"Oh, Thonk—Yoou. Com. Way." With his tightened, crippled hands he pointed up the street. Christy pushed and pushed and pushed some more. A mile up the hill, four more curbs, and two mud puddles later, Jordan signaled her to turn left into an apartment garage and stop at the elevator door.

"Com, in" he said. Christy, with nose hairs frozen, ears ringing, and a hypothermic posture, couldn't resist the invitation to dry off and thaw out before she started the arctic trek back to her car.

As they entered his apartment, Jordan immediately wheeled into the back bedroom. Christy followed to find Jordan leaning over the bed, talking to an elderly woman. "Ma-Mom," Jordan smiled and proudly confessed. "Ah-tak-car-of-her. She-ma-he-ro."

As Christy warmed up outside and inside, it became easier for her to understand his words and his heart. In total awe and amazement, Christy discovered Jordan had been taking care of his mother since she had a stroke four years ago.

Christy also discovered Jordan was a senior in school like her. This was also his last day of school, and he too would graduate. She also discovered he had read one book per week every week for the last four years and that he spoke five languages. More amazing was the fact he had never missed a day of school since he was a freshman.

Every day of college, for the last four years, Jordan had pushed himself more than a mile each way, up and down the hill, to and from class, to and from school. His apartment was the only handicapped accessible building in close proximity to the campus, which left him no other choice but to live there. His father had passed away, he was an only child, and when his mother took ill, he had her move in with him three weeks after school had started.

An hour passed by quickly, and as Christy got up to leave, Jordan reached out for her hand. With tears in his eyes Jordan slowly whispered, "Thonk—You. In ma whole laff, nev-er, en-ee-bo-dy push ma wheeeel-chor. Mos pop-ple scared of ma. Ah diff-er-ont, not stu-pid, jus diff-er-ont on out-sod. In-sod ah hav dree-ms jus lak ev-er-ee-bo-dy el-se. In-sod I lov an need to be needed. Som God who ma-ke them, ma-ke me too. Thonk-you, Thonk-you."

Jordan then wheeled over to a table and picked up a Bible. Dedicated to being gentle and careful not to tear it or drop it, he struggled to open it and find the right page. Finally he pointed at 1 Samuel 16:7 and said, "Reeed."

The dim, gloomy day had suddenly changed. Christy had no more pain of backache, fatigue, and blisters—no more excuses. *It's amazing,* she thought, *how when you surround yourself with light it, brightens up you and your day.* The long walk back to her car seemed short and quick as Christy warmed to the thoughts of Jordan, his predicament, and his positive, passionate understanding of what life, personal achievement, lasting success, and loving relationships are really all about. Jordan was getting a bachelor's degree in English, but he already had a PhD in life.

Of all the lessons Christy learned in four years of college and in all the hours spent studying the required curriculum, she learned the most powerful, profound lesson on her last day of school: "Look not at his countenance or on the height of his stature. For the Lord seeth not as man seeth. Man looketh on the outward appearance, but the Lord looketh on the heart."

Perspective

What Makes You an American?

What did you learn about America when the terrorists attacked us on September 11, 2001?

U.S. President Dwight D. Eisenhower said, "Whatever America hopes to bring to pass in the world must first come to pass in the heart of Americans. Freedom has its life in the hearts, the actions, and in the spirit of men and women, so it must be daily earned and refreshed—else, like a flower cut from its life-giving roots, it will wither and die."

If you agree, let me ask you: Are you contributing to or living off of the government? We have a Bill of Rights. We need a Bill of Responsibility. Unless you buy into the full concept of constitutional democracy, which is rule-of-law freedom with responsibility to protect the rights of every single person; unless you buy into a capitalist, free-market economic system and especially religious freedom—a separation of church and state and equality for women in religion, politics, and society—*living in America does not make you an American.*

The nineteen Muslim hijackers who attacked us on September 11 were residents living in our country, buying and eating our wonderful selection of foods, taking flying lessons from our extraordinary schools, and partaking of our clean water, clean air, lack of disease, and world-class health care. These Muslim fundamentalists even partook of our sleazy strip clubs in Las Vegas while they planned their sick attacks on us American "infidels."

So what are we to learn? These terrorists did not attack our country, a landmass, buildings, or people. They attacked what we believe in. And no, they didn't attack a symbol of minimum requirement, or mediocrity, or a sense of entitlement. They attacked symbols of our freedom and symbols of the opportunities we have to take advantage of that freedom.

On a more positive note, this is not a slam on the "unregistered" people living in America who are here illegally. Rather, this is a wake-up call for any one of us who takes America for granted.

A friend of mine in New Mexico hired two young men to come into his McDonald's restaurant after hours to clean the bathrooms and make the eating area spit-spot before the customers arrived the next morning. Both of these young men were in America illegally and neither of them spoke a word of English, but for minimum wage workers, my friend said he had never found anyone who worked harder than these two men. They always arrived early and stayed late, if necessary, to get their jobs done.

These men came to America to better themselves and to provide a better life for their families. They understood what America represents and wanted to be a part of her. Consequently, they didn't just sit around content to be what they were. They went to work each night visualizing what they had the power to become, taught themselves how to speak and write fluent English, and enrolled in school to learn about business, finance, and how the American free enterprise system works. They went through the proper steps to obtain U.S. citizenship, and now both of them own their own McDonald's franchises, with a conviction that living in America does not make you an American. America is a belief and a set of high ideals couched in incentive motivation to give it everything we've got when less would be sufficient.

I fly on Delta Airlines and hold their highest Diamond Medallion status, which means I have access to their customer service hotline, called Special Member Services. One day in 2010, my flight into Reagan National Airport in Washington, D.C., was canceled. When I phoned the special number for emergency VIP help, a polite, professional woman greeted me by name and asked how she could help me. I explained my crisis and what I needed her to do. She said, "I'm sorry, Mr. Clark, I can't do that."

In the past, I would have used my persuasive skills to explain that she shouldn't allow "can't" to mean "won't," and that her refusal to help me was a choice she didn't have to make. Where there's a will, there's always a *won't*, but there's always a way—she just needed to find it. But not once have I ever been successful at getting a customer service agent to change his or her mind, so I didn't waste any time.

Instead, I asked her which call center she was working at and she answered, "Cincinnati." I said, "Thank you," hung up the telephone, and immediately called back the same special number. A different woman answered, politely and professionally greeted me by name, and asked the same question: "How may I help you?" I explained my exact same crisis and made the same request. She said, "No problem, Mr. Clark. I can do that."

Both customer service agents had gone through the same training and had access to the same software, computer screens, and solutions. One said no, and the other said yes. One was complacent and took her job for granted; the other appreciated her employment, took pride in her career, and in some measure viewed her relationship with customers as a one-way, covenant kind of arrangement. I was in a huge hurry, but I asked this second customer service agent to tell me her location. With a beautiful, barely noticeable accent, she replied, "India." In light of this entitlement-versus-opportunity scenario, is it really a mystery why so many American jobs are moving to foreign countries?

You Can if You Think You Can

In December 1982, my dear friend Bob Coyne of Brantford, Ontario, decided to host a junior hockey team from Sweden. In exchange, the members of Bob's Canadian junior team would travel to Sweden the following year as guests of the Swedish team. The team from Sweden arrived in Canada on Boxing Day (December 26). This team was the pride and joy of Stockholm. It consisted of fourteen- and fifteen-year-old boys, handpicked from Stockholm and its vicinity, and was reputed to be a notoriously tough hockey club. As hosts, Bob and his team were to provide the Swedish team with a tour of each of the seven different communities where it would play its seven exhibition games. The final game was to be between the Stockholm team and Bob's Brantford team.

Upon arriving in Canada, the Stockholm team's hope, of course, was to win all seven games and return home with grand tales of victory. It was the first time away from home for these kids. They were suffering from jet lag, and they lost their first game by a dismal 8–1 score. It was a staggering defeat for them. They were a little more prepared for the second game, but again they lost, this time 4–2. They lost the third and fourth games as well. The fifth game was a devastating 9–1 lashing.

At this point in the tour, which was somewhere around New Year's Day, Bob decided they needed a break in the action, a diversion to rally their confidence and rebuild their self-esteem. He arranged a visit to Toronto to see the CN Tower, the National Hockey League Hall of Fame, and other points of interest. The Swedish team would play no hockey for two entire days, but could swim and play basketball at a local high school for entertainment and exercise.

At the end of the Toronto trip, Bob took them to the student center to sit and relax while they waited for the bus to pick them up and take them back to their sponsoring homes. The coach of the Stockholm team asked Bob if there was something he could say to his team that might psych them up for the next game.

Bob was neither prepared nor thinking in those terms, but he decided, on the spur of the moment, to see if he could touch their emotions.

Bob started talking to them about home, which got them right up off their chairs. He asked them if they missed their moms and dads and if the time change was bothering them. Bob explained that in Stockholm, there were fewer daylight hours during the winter than there were in Canada, and surely this change was affecting them. Bob finally steered the conversation toward hockey, reflecting on their five losses in a row, which surely was not typical of the team, and how they all must feel about these losses. Bob concluded by suggesting that what they needed was something to which they could reach out and relate. He told them that all they needed was the confidence to believe in themselves again. So he left them with a phrase he had heard many other times: "You can if you think you can." Bob then repeated this phrase to each kid individually while he looked each one squarely in the eye. When he had repeated the phrase to each one of them, he left the room. A few moments later, the bus arrived and they all left.

Bob really didn't think he had convinced them, but he went home prepared to reinforce the idea anyway. He made a big sign bearing the phrase YOU CAN IF YOU THINK YOU CAN and took it with him to the next game, which was held at the Six Nations Indian Reservation just south of Francis. Six Nations had a top-notch hockey club, and the Stockholm team knew it. Even prior to arriving in Canada, the Stockholm team was prepared that if it lost a game, it would be either to Six Nations or to Brantford.

Game time arrived, and the Swedish team was still in the locker room. They didn't appear to be coming out, so Bob went in to see what was happening. Most of the team members hung their heads while their coach addressed them, and Bob could see they just weren't up for the game. They turned to look at Bob when he barged in. He smiled broadly and said, "Remember, you can if you think you can!" He waved to the Swedish coach and swiftly exited the locker room.

Bob then hung the sign he had made, unbeknownst to the Swedish team, on the back of their team bench. A minute later, the Swedish team emerged and saw the sign. Spontaneously, every member of the team touched the sign. From there, they went out onto the ice, warmed up, and then faced off to open the game.

Very early on, they took a 1–0 lead, and again they all jumped the boards, touched the sign, and went back out for the face-off. The game continued. The Swedish team scored another goal and again, each member of the team touched the sign. Six Nations came back to tie the game, but for those kids who hadn't won a single game during their entire tour, the tie was as good as a win. The tie put them on top of the world. The noise during the bus ride home was unbelievable!

That brings us to the last day of the tournament. Bob's Brantford team was the Stockholm team's last opponent. He had arranged to pick up the Stockholm team's coach at his hotel room for a pregame lunch. When Bob entered the coach's room, he saw the YOU CAN IF YOU THINK YOU CAN sign propped up on the headboard of the bed. Bob thought it was kind of funny, but he could see that the Stockholm coach really believed it because, as they left for the arena, he grabbed the sign to hang over the bench.

When the Swedish team came onto the ice, they performed the same ritual as they had at Six Nations, each player touched the sign before the start of the game. This final game of the series was a highly competitive, spirited contest and Stockholm beat Brantford by two points. Every time the Swedish team scored, they touched the sign and also skated past Bob's bench grinning and triumphantly shaking their fists at him. There was a party for the team after the game ended, and the next morning, the players flew home to Stockholm.

The following December, Bob's team arrived in Stockholm for the exchange tournament. The setup for sports in Sweden is different from the setup in Canada. The Swedes have sports clubs for almost every sport, but all the clubs play in the same arena. The sports building is in downtown Stockholm, and Bob and his junior team went there for a reception following their arrival in Sweden. As they entered the main lobby of the huge, city-owned, government-operated arena, Bob noticed the YOU CAN IF YOU THINK YOU CAN sign hanging on the wall about twelve feet from the floor. The sign was framed, and beneath it was an inscription of the story of its origin and impact. Bob was surprised, happy, and choked up all at the same time.

To this day, that sign still graces the lobby of the Stockholm sports complex, teaching the value of the power of positive thinking to all who enter!

Shmily

My grandparents were married for more than half a century and played their own special game from the time they had met each other. The goal of their game was to write the word "shmily" in a surprise place for the other to find.

They took turns leaving "shmily" around the house, and as soon as one of them discovered it, it was their turn to hide it once more. They dragged "shmily" with their fingers through the sugar and flour containers to await whoever was preparing the next meal. They smeared it in the dew on the windows overlooking the patio where my grandma always fed us warm homemade pudding with blue food coloring.

"Shmily" was written in the steam left on the mirror after a hot shower, where it would reappear bath after bath. At one point, my grandmother even unrolled an entire roll of toilet paper to leave "shmily" on the very last sheet.

There was no end to the places "shmily" would pop up. Little notes with "shmily" scribbled hurriedly were found on dashboards and car seats or taped to steering wheels. The notes were stuffed inside shoes and left traced in the ashes of the fireplace. This mysterious word was as much a part of my grandparents' house as the furniture.

It took me a long time before I was able to fully appreciate my grandparents' game. Skepticism has kept me from believing in true love, one that is pure and enduring. However, I never doubted my grandparents' relationship. They had love down pat. It was more than their flirtatious little games; it was a way of life. Their relationship was based on a devotion and passionate affection, which not everyone is lucky enough to experience. Grandma and Grandpa held hands every chance they could. They stole kisses as they bumped into each other in their tiny kitchen. They finished each other's sentences and shared the daily crossword puzzle and word jumble. My grandma whispered to me about how cute my grandpa was, how handsome and old he had grown to be. She claimed that she really knew "how to pick 'em." Before every meal, they bowed their heads and gave thanks, marveling at their blessings: a wonderful family, good fortune, and each other.

But there was a dark cloud in my grandparents' life: my grandmother had breast cancer. The disease had first appeared ten years earlier. As always, Grandpa was with her every step of the way. He comforted her in their yellow room, painted that way so she could always be surrounded by sunshine, even when she was too sick to go outside.

Now the cancer was again attacking her body. With the help of a cane and my grandfather's steady hand, they went to church every morning. But my grandmother grew steadily weaker until, finally, she could not leave the house anymore. For a while, Grandpa would go to church alone, praying to God to watch over his wife. Then one day, what we all dreaded finally happened. Grandma was gone.

"Shmily." It was scrawled in yellow on the pink ribbons of my grandmother's funeral bouquet. As the crowd thinned and the last mourners turned to leave, my aunts, uncles, cousins, and other family members came forward and gathered around Grandma one last time. Grandpa stepped up to my grandmother's casket, and taking a shaky breath, he began to sing to her.

Through his tears and grief, the song came, a deep and throaty lullaby. Shaking with my own sorrow, I will never forget that moment. For I knew that although I couldn't begin to fathom the depth of their love, I had been privileged to witness its unmatched beauty. He sweetly sang as we all should: " S-h-m-i-l-y: See How Much I Love You."

Champions See the Goal

In 1980, Eric Heiden won five Olympic gold medals and set five world records as a speed skater. For four years prior to the Olympics, he practiced four hours a day, six days a week. Because of the brutal winters, much of his training was on an indoor stationary skating machine.

An ABC television crew went to Wisconsin to film these special training sessions. The camera focused on the incredible intensity, rhythm, and determination. Heiden's strength and finesse were unbelievable. One might have expected Heiden's face to be strained and grimacing. But there was no anguish, no complaining—just a smile.

Staged for the camera?

No. What we did not see on the screen, but what was in full view of Heiden, was a giant picture of five gold medals. Heiden could see the gold medals the entire time he practiced. When fatigue set in, he visualized and imagined what he would feel like when he won them.

Any champion, like Eric Heiden, willingly pays the price to win. They know the benefits of winning are worth the effort. This is the third step to becoming a champion. First, see yourself as a winner. Second, discipline yourself to become one. Third, be willing to pay the price in hard work.

Illegitimi Non Carborundum

Have you ever had a tough day? How about a rough month? Can you imagine twelve months of pure hell? The next time you think you have it bad, remember that neither success nor failure means anything in and of itself—the meaning of both emerges only in comparison to something or someone else. For this reason, I want to introduce you to one of the greatest men who ever lived.

Donald C. Sansom graduated high school at the age of seventeen. On his eighteenth birthday, February 25, 1943, he was eligible to enlist in the US Army Air Corps. The United States was in the middle of World War II, and Don wanted to do his part and serve his country. On April 7, Don left on a troop train headed for preflight officer training school in Santa Ana, California.

That December, Don graduated third in his class of 130 servicemen, and at eighteen years of age, he was the youngest second lieutenant in the US Army Air Corps.

Overseas training took place in Sioux City, Iowa, and in April 1944, Don left for North Africa. On the morning of D-Day, when the Allied forces stormed the Normandy beaches, Don boarded a troopship bound for Italy. The message broadcast over the ship's public address system instructed every soldier to meet on deck in fifteen minutes. More than four thousand soldiers stood at attention as the commander addressed them. "Men, we are headed into war," he said solemnly. "Right now the Allies are flying one thousand plane raids into Germany every single day." He then continued, "Using simple arithmetic, we can calculate that with ten crewmen aboard each of these bombers, we are losing between five hundred and one thousand men every day. This means that within the week, more than one-third of you could either be dead or captured. I don't know about you, but

I think we should change these odds. Look around. Let's commit to one another right here and now to never say never. We shall change the odds. We shall win this conflict. We shall win it for our families, for our country, for the free world! God bless each of you for standing up for what's right. God bless America!" He then concluded with the mock "Latin" phrase *Illegitimi non carborundum.*

Don couldn't hold back the tears that welled up as he felt for the first time the true meaning of duty, pride, and honor. The loud cheers of the soldiers echoed in his mind and heart for days afterward. Finally they arrived in Italy, and Don was assigned to fly with the squadron commander. Because of his exceptional skill and proven leadership abilities, Don was named the lead bombardier in a B-17 flown by Deke Davies.

Don felt great about his chances for survival, for Deke's reputation was legendary. Deke had already flown forty-nine missions, returning with his planes shot up, ripped apart, missing their engines, and on fire. But somehow, he always found a way to bring his plane and crew back safely.

The next morning would be Don's first bombing mission and Deke's last prior to being rotated home to receive a true hero's welcome. They took off and were flying over Budapest, Hungary. Don was sitting in the bombardier's seat under the nose of the aircraft when they were severely hit by enemy fire. Engine number one was blown apart, and engine number two was on fire. With only two of four engines functioning, they finished the mission, successfully hit their target, and turned around to head back to the base. Halfway back to base, they lost fuel and altitude and crash-landed in a wheat field in Yugoslavia.

Try to imagine the emotions Don's family must have felt upon receiving the news that he was missing in action. The news that he was alive and of his whereabouts wasn't released for another six months. His friends and loved ones wondered whether he would ever come home.

German soldiers immediately pulled up in trucks and opened machine-gun fire on the wreckage. Don ignited the plane in order to destroy the equipment and documents as he and his nine fellow crew members scattered for cover. The Germans quickly captured the entire crew except for Don and two others, who managed to elude the enemy for more than two hours by crawling on their bellies through the field. Finally they made it to a road at the end of the farmland. The peasants working alongside it pointed to a small nearby bridge underneath which Don and his comrades could hide. When Don heard the *clomp* of the soldiers as they marched across the bridge, he thought he and his two comrades were safe—the enemy soldiers had suspended their search and were heading back to base. But wouldn't you know it? The last soldier had to relieve himself and stepped down the embankment for some privacy. He inadvertently looked under the bridge and saw the American airmen crouched in the shadows. He started screaming, and within seconds Don and his comrades were surrounded with enemy machine guns pointed at their heads. Don's copilot pulled out a white handkerchief, waved it in surrender, and reminded his fellow airmen of their commander's words, *Illegitimi non carborundum.* Don and the others were immediately stripped and put in a local farmer's pigpen together with the pigs, mud, and muck. They were guarded for two weeks until they were transferred by train to Frankfurt, Germany, for interrogation. After one week in solitary confinement, they were transferred to Stalag Luft 3, a German prison camp for airmen of the Allies. The day prior to the arrival of Don and his comrades, the Germans had captured and brutally executed fifty prisoners who were trying to escape. It was this prisoner-of-war camp that inspired the film *The Great Escape* and the television series *Hogan's Heroes.*

When winter came, Don and his fellow prisoners were forced on death marches in fifteen to twenty degrees below zero temperatures and blizzard conditions. These marches spanned eighty-five miles and lasted three days. The cold was so fierce that many prisoners froze to death, literally dying as they marched. They eventually left this camp in northeastern Germany on the Baltic Sea and marched one last time across Germany to its southwestern corner, where they stopped at a huge installation called Stalag 7A. Ten thousand soldiers were incarcerated at this single location. Sustaining motivation and personal dignity while enduring torture and starvation would have been nearly impossible except for the tiny inspirational reminder Don's copilot had carved in the latrine door: *Illegitimi non carborundum.*

Don and his fellow prisoners remained in this camp until it was finally liberated on April 29, 1945, by Patton's Seventh Army Tank Battalion, which had just won a battle in a small village next to the camp. Don was sent to France for the rehabilitation of his sickly and weakened 129-pound body. He was released at a healthier 170 pounds and allowed to return home to the states. During the three weeks of his rehabilitation, Don had time to focus on his dreams and set personal and educational goals. It was during that time that he set his professional sights on becoming a dentist.

In 1946, while attending the University of Utah as a student in the pre-dentistry program, he fell in love with the beautiful, talented, and artistic Barbara Sims. They married and headed for Kansas City in 1947 for Don to attend dental school. Over the years, they became the proud parents of six children and settled in Utah to raise their family. Donald C. Sansom was affectionately known to his family and hundreds of admiring friends as "Doc" and ran one of the largest and most successful dental practices in the Intermountain West. But he was especially known for his amazing love of life. Don was the legendary "Silver Fox" of the Snowbird Ski Resort and could out-ski anyone else on the mountain. He was an amazing water skier and golfer as well. Most important to him, though, were the scores of young people he taught how to snow ski, water ski, golf, mountain bike, hike, and be fully alive!

Many people only look forward to Friday instead of Monday. They hate their jobs and think they are paid for attendance instead of productivity. Not Don. And why not Don? His glass was never half empty. His worth ethic was never one of half measure. His love of freedom and respect for America was never halfhearted, and his ability to bounce back was never half-cocked. Since the day he first heard the phrase on the troopship and again underneath the enemy bridge when he was captured in war, and when he saw it on a daily basis on the prison camp latrine door, that phrase served as his rallying cry, helping him to persevere and to help others do the same. In fact, he claimed the phrase as the official dental motto. Regardless of whether he was dealing with a negative patient, a black diamond ski run, a cold mountain lake during a weekend of water-skiing, or a deep sand trap in the golf course rough, Don "Doc" Sansom grinned and won by understanding: *Illegitimi non carborundum*—Don't let the bastards grind you down!

Questions and Answers

My college professor asked his students to list what we thought were the Seven Wonders of the World. Out of the hundred students in the lecture hall, the general consensus was:

1. Egypt's pyramids
2. Great Wall of China
3. Grand Canyon
4. Taj Mahal
5. Rainbow Bridge at Arches National Monument
6. Niagara Falls
7. Geysers in Yellowstone Park
8. (St. Peter's Basilica and the Golden Gate Bridge were also mentioned.)

While gathering the votes, the professor noted that one student had not yet finished her paper. He asked the girl if she was having trouble answering the question. She replied, "No, I'm not having trouble with the answer; I'm having trouble with the question. Why only seven? According to whom and what criteria? What does 'wonder' mean to you, and is it different for me?"

The professor responded, "Tell us what you have, and maybe we can help." The girl hesitated and then read, "I think the real Seven Wonders of the World are to see, to hear, to taste, to touch, to laugh, to feel, and to love."

The room was so quiet you could have heard a pin drop. The professor took a deep breath and replied, "Wow! This is the most profound lesson we will learn all year. And isn't it pathetic that out of the 101 people in this room—me included—that only one of us, only 1 percent, understands that the things we overlook as simple and fundamental truly are wondrous?"

This story provides three powerful reminders:

- The most important and precious things in life cannot be bought or built by hand.
- Before we look for answers outside of ourselves, let us first look within.
- Life is not about answers; it's about questions.

If you really analyze it, life is nothing more than just a string of back-to-back questions linked together and fueled by our curiosity and commitment to uncover the whole truth. Only when we ask the right questions can we get the right answers and progress to the next right question.

For example, in the corporate world, the popular culture thing to do is to publish organizational "mission" and "vision" statements, make a list of "core values," and solicit "commitment." To do so requires the correct questions. A mission statement answers, "Why do we exist?" A vision statement answers, "What do we want to be?" Values clarification answers, "What will we do?" Personal commitment answers, "What will I do?"

Significance

One Moment in Time

One day, Henry Winkler, the actor best known for his portrayal of Fonzie on the television series *Happy Days,* decided to take some time off and treat himself to a matinee movie. To avoid fans making a fuss over him, Winkler entered the theater from the side exit door. He shuffled his way into an aisle and found himself a vacant seat.

As Henry turned around to sit down, the little girl sitting in the row behind him smiled broadly, pointed her finger, and slowly said, "Fonzie." Winkler immediately snapped into the Fonzie character, flipping his hair, swiveling his hips, and glancing left and right.

In his signature pose he then pointed his finger at the girl and said, "Whoa!" To everyone's surprise, the lady sitting next to the little girl passed out.

The theater manager went out to assist the woman. Lying in the aisle with a cold pack on her forehead, the woman was asked one question: "Why did you pass out?"

Pointing to the little girl, she replied, "My daughter is autistic, and that is the very first word she has ever spoken in her entire life!"

Rescue at Sea

My grandfather spent a lot of time in the Netherlands where he witnessed a legendary tale. In a small fishing village in Holland, a young boy taught the world about the rewards of unselfish service. Because the entire village revolved around the fishing industry, a volunteer rescue team was needed in cases of emergency. One night the winds raged, the clouds burst, and a gale-force storm capsized a fishing boat at sea. Stranded and in trouble, the crew sent out the SOS. The captain of the rescue rowboat team sounded the alarm, and the villagers assembled in the town square overlooking the bay. While the team launched their rowboat and fought their way through the wild waves, the villagers waited restlessly on the beach, holding lanterns to light the way back.

An hour later, the rescue boat reappeared through the fog, and the cheering villagers ran to greet them. Falling exhausted on the sand, the volunteers reported that the rescue boat could not hold anymore passengers, and they had to leave one man behind. Even one more passenger would have surely capsized the rescue boat, and all would have been lost.

Frantically, the captain called for another volunteer team to go after the lone survivor. Sixteen-year-old Hans stepped forward. His mother grabbed his arm, pleading, "Please don't go. Your father died in a shipwreck ten years ago, and your older brother, Peter, has been lost at sea for three weeks. Hans, you are all I have left."

Hans replied, "Mother, I have to go. What if everyone said, 'I can't go, let someone else do it'? Mother, this time I have to do my duty. When the call for service comes, we all need to take our turn and do our part." Hans kissed his mother, joined the team, and disappeared into the night.

Another hour passed, which seemed to Hans's mother like an eternity. Finally, the rescue boat darted through the fog. Hans was standing up in the bow. Cupping his hands, the captain called, "Did you find the lost man?" Barely able to contain himself, Hans excitedly yelled back, "Yes, we found him. And tell my mother it's my older brother, Peter!"

Stride to Be Better

I was in Maui, Hawaii, on vacation when Naomi Rhode, a professional speaker, taught me about high expectations. She and her husband, Jim, had been walking along the beach for several hundred yards when she paused to look back to see how far they had gone. She noticed their footprints in the sand and was immediately filled with pride. She pointed them out to her husband and commented, "Wow, think about how many times we have left our footprints in the lives of others."

Suddenly the ocean interrupted by sweeping in and washing away their footprints, leaving no sign of their presence. Naomi was puzzled and almost hurt. She asked her husband, "How can we leave a more lasting impression on people that will not be washed away with time?"

He wisely replied, "Just walk on higher ground."

A Brother Like That

As a preacher, Dr. C. Roy Angell thought he understood the true meaning of friendship and love. Then it happened. His friend Paul received an automobile from his brother as a Christmas present. On Christmas Eve when Paul came out of his office, a street urchin was walking around the shiny new car, admiring it. "Is this your car, Mister?" he asked.

Paul nodded. "My brother gave it to me for Christmas." The boy was astounded. "You mean your brother gave it to you and it didn't cost you nothing? Boy, I wish ..." He hesitated.

Of course Paul knew what he was going to wish for. He was going to wish he had a brother like that. But what the lad said jarred Paul all the way down to his heels.

"I wish," the boy went on, "that I could be a brother like that."

Paul looked at the boy in astonishment. Then he impulsively added, "Would you like to take a ride in my automobile?"

"Oh yes, I'd love that."

After a short ride, the boy turned and with his eyes aglow said, "Mister, would you mind driving in front of my house?"

Paul smiled a little. He thought he knew what the lad wanted. He wanted to show his neighbors that he could ride home in a big automobile. But Paul was wrong again. "Will you stop where those two steps are?" the boy asked.

He ran up the steps. Then in a little while Paul heard him coming back, but he was not coming fast. He was carrying his little crippled brother. He sat him down on the bottom step, then sort of squeezed up against him and pointed to the car.

"There she is, Buddy, just like I told you upstairs. His brother gave it to him for Christmas and it didn't cost him a cent. And someday I'm gonna give you one just like it . . . then you can see for yourself all the pretty things in the Christmas windows that I've been trying to tell you about."

Paul got out and lifted the lad to the front seat of his car. The shining-eyed older brother climbed in beside him and the three of them began a memorable holiday ride.

That Christmas Eve, Paul and Roy both learned what Jesus meant when he said, "It is more blessed to give . . ."

An Educational System

In my sophomore year of high school, I met the anthropology teacher, Mr. Croft. I was a tall, gangly, insecure kid who only went to class to stay eligible for athletic competition. I didn't know anything about anthropology except that "we came from the goo, went through the zoo, and now we're you, whoop-dee-doo," so I never signed up for Mr. Croft's class. The intriguing thing about this is that it didn't stop him from positively impacting my life.

Mr. Croft was a teacher twenty-four hours a day—in the grocery store on Saturday, in the park on Sunday afternoon, after school, before school, and in and out of his classroom. Mr. Croft inspired and taught every student at East High, especially me. He encouraged me to become all I could possibly be.

How could I possibly repay Mr. Croft?

A few years after I graduated from high school, I had an opportunity to coach Pop Warner football for thirteen-year-olds who had never played before. To get a feel for the boys' abilities, I lined them up into two rows and had each of them run out for a pass. I wanted to see who could run, catch, and throw so I could formulate a team in my mind.

Two days into practice, a tall, gangly, insecure kid wearing a new shirt, new jeans, and new loafers showed up on the field. I asked him if he didn't want to go home and change his clothes. He boldly replied, "I've already missed two days of practice, and I don't want to miss anymore. I came to play ball!"

He got in line, and when he ran out for a pass, I threw the ball. It hit him square in the head. He picked up the ball and ran it back to me. He slapped it into my chest and ran to the other line. It came time for his second pass and I hit him in the head again. With his nose bleeding and his lip swelling, he picked up the ball, raced it back to me, and got back in line.

134

On his third attempt, I lofted a soft, easy pass, but it was over his head. He dove for the ball, but came up nowhere near it. Covered with grass stains from head to toe, his body messy, mucky, and soaking wet, he got up, took the muddy ball, raced back to me, and slapped it to my chest.

Figuring I'd better have a chat with him before he killed himself, I pulled him out of line and asked, "Why are you here? Does your dad want you to be a football star? Did your friends talk you into it?"

He looked up with his big brown eyes and said, "Coach, I'm here because I want to play football. And I promise if you'll help me, I know I can do it!"

"What's your name?" I asked.

He shyly answered, "Tommy Croft."

Shocked, I asked if his dad taught anthropology at East High School. Surprised, he replied, "I think so."

"Get back in line," I told him. Here, at last, was my chance to be a Mr. Croft to a Croft! Here was my chance to give something back. For the first time in my life, I understood the meaning of "an educational system." What goes around really does come around!

People Are Watching

It's not enough to shake the hand of a man or woman in military uniform and say thanks. Our troops have been at war for nineteen years while we've been at the mall! It's not enough to put a magnetic sign on the side of our vehicles that says "Support Our Troops" and feel like we're doing our part. That's why I made a commitment many years ago that whenever I saw a soldier, airman, sailor, or marine in an airport, I would buy him or her a meal. What a drag! No one told me they don't hang out by themselves. They're always in groups of three, five, ten. I'm going broke!

Because winning isn't a sometime thing, it's an all-the-time thing, and because service before self is a governing core value that we don't turn off and on, I also needed to take this same commitment on board my flights.

I always fly first class (Delta Airlines takes great care of me), and I always get a window seat. One day I was seated, drinks had been served, and the other passengers started to board the plane. As the slower moving people caused congestion in the aisle, a soldier in his combat uniform was stopped at my row. So, I chatted him up.

"How are you?"

"I'm fine, Sir."

"Are you coming or going?"

"I'm coming back from the desert, Sir."

They are always so polite. I said, "I bet you are excited to see your family."

He said, "Yes, Sir, I've been in Iraq for fifteen months, and I hope they are excited to see me."

I said, "Guaranteed, bro! Welcome home," and offered him my seat.

He replied, "No, thank you, Sir, that's not necessary."

I said, "What do you mean it's not necessary? It's the least I can do. C'mon, swap seats with me." I stood up and he reluctantly slid in to sit down. The flight attendant acknowledged how cool she thought this was, to which I responded that it was the least any of us could do and to take good care of him and give him anything he wants.

As I moved to the back of the plane to find his seat, wouldn't you know it? He had a middle seat between two chubby guys. I'm six foot five and weigh 235 pounds! Both guys were looking at me like, "Oh no!" I was wincing back "Oh, yes."

As I sat down and squished my body in between them, it was easy to feel sorry for myself. It was a four hour flight and this was not what I had in mind. I felt like I had sat on a stick and my immediate discomfort flipped my positive commitment to service before self to a self-centered negative focus on what was wrong. I silently complained, "I'm so old that I bend over to pull up my socks and think, what else can I accomplish while I'm way down here?" I go to bed healthy and wake up injured, and all I did was lie there! My hip hurts, my foot is asleep, I limp for five minutes until I stop shaking, and now I'm stuck between Bubba and Blubba!

Then I remembered when I was in Baghdad. It was 140 degrees Fahrenheit, and on top of this, our soldiers, airmen, sailors, and marines are wearing eight-five pounds of combat gear while living and working in harm's way with no opportunities to take a day off. They are running toward the sound of guns, willing to sacrifice their lives if necessary, so we can live with the peace of mind that we are safe and free.

How dare I complain about a sore back or go home from work because the air conditioner broke or take my freedom for granted! Suddenly, I stopped treating my fellow seatmates as objects and started talking to them as human beings. Everything was going to be fine. Then it happened.

The gentleman who was sitting next to me in first class came wandering to the back of the plane. When we made eye contact, I acknowledged him with a "What's up?" He replied, "You made us all stop and think. When the next soldier got on the plane, I gave him my seat." I smiled and replied, "Let me help you find yours."

Wouldn't you know it? He was seated in the row right in front of me in the center seat between two chubbier guys! He was so stuck he couldn't even turn around to keep complaining! Before we took off, four of us who had been sitting in first class were now sitting in the back of the plane to pay tribute to four soldiers who we should always honor, assist, and support.

But the story doesn't stop here. I checked into my hotel, had a great night's sleep, awoke refreshed and alert, put on my coat and tie, and entered the huge ballroom as the keynote speaker. Wouldn't you know it? The CEO who introduced me was the gentleman who was sitting next to me in first class. He read my standard introduction and then acknowledged to his 5,000 employees that I had inspired him and his colleagues to give up their seats to say thank you to our soldiers.

What is the moral to this story? People are watching. We are the message. It is not enough to just practice what we preach, we must preach everywhere we practice!

Overcoming

At age fourteen, Michael Dowling fell from the back of a wagon in a blizzard. Before his parents realized it and returned to find him, he had been severely frostbitten. Both of his legs had to be amputated, one at the hip, the other at the knee. His right arm and left hand were amputated as well. When he came out of surgery and examined what was left of his body, Michael was so depressed he said he wanted to commit suicide, but he couldn't figure out how to do it. Over time, he snapped out of it and went to the board of county commissioners and told them if they would buy him some artificial limbs and educate him, he would pay them back in full. They fulfilled his request.

Years later, during World War II, the army sent Michael to Europe to visit wounded soldiers. Standing in a hotel, he spoke to a large group of bedridden men that had lost an eye, a leg, or an arm. He began to minimize the seriousness of their wounds, and the soldiers were getting upset. In fact, they began to boo him. In response, Michael began to walk toward them and told them to set high goals for themselves and not to feel sorry for themselves. The enraged soldiers then yelled obscenities at him. Finally, he sat down on a chair and took off his right leg. The soldiers calmed down a bit, but they still resented him. Then he took off his left leg. The booing stopped but Michael didn't. He took off his right arm, flipped off his left hand, and there he sat, a stump of a body. Now that he had their attention, Dowling delivered a speech on taking personal responsibility for success through goal setting and turning lemons into lemonade.

You see, Michael Dowling had become the president of one of the largest banks in Minnesota, a father of five, and the U.S. Chamber of Commerce Man of the Year.

Wild Man

Most teachers are loving, considerate, supportive, positive individuals. But, as in any profession, there are always negative people who spread negative energy and gossip about others.

Years ago, when I arrived to speak at a high school convocation in Louisiana, I entered the faculty lounge to relax and get my thoughts together. Two teachers stormed through the door and immediately started griping about a student I'll call the Wild Man.

"That long-haired, dope-smoking, Frisbee-throwing, skateboard-jumping, flag-burning hippie will never amount to a hill of beans," said one. The other joined in with ridiculous gossip about as accurate as "My wife's sister's dog's mother-in-law told me through the grapevine that he did this and that."

When I couldn't take the negative comments any longer, I found the auditorium and checked out the sound system. There I met the very positive, professional principal who explained the plan for the day.

There was a student in the school who had been a friend to everyone. Zachary was an energetic kid who supported all the games and dances. He had multiple sclerosis—a disease that affects the nerves and muscles. For years Zach had been in a manual wheelchair, moving from class to class and function to function.

A month before I arrived, Zach's condition worsened and he needed a motorized wheelchair to stay at this school. Without it, he would have to attend a school with special equipment.

It turned out that Zach couldn't afford the new electric chair, so his only choice was to check out. Today was the day Zach was leaving; he was in the counselor's office with his parents filling out the final paperwork.

The school assembly was announced and Zach and his parents were casually invited into the auditorium. The students and faculty filled the giant room and Zach took his usual spot out in the aisle on the fifteenth row. Zach assumed it was his last day and last event at this school. Before they introduced me as the speaker, the real drama unfolded.

The student body president was introduced and he came onstage for the Pledge of Allegiance. He then shocked everyone when he introduced Wild Man—the kid the teachers were degrading in the faculty lounge. With green hair, numerous rings in his ear, and two fly-fishing hooks in his eyebrow, Wild Man caused a stir among the teachers.

Without saying a word, Wild Man gave a signal and four football players approached Zach, lifted him out of the wheelchair, and brought him to the center of the stage. Wild Man gave another signal and two students from the band presented Zach's parents with flowers and escorted them to the stage.

Wild Man then excused himself and disappeared backstage. Seconds later, he reappeared driving a brand-new, shiny, chrome-plated electric wheelchair with a giant bow in the school colors taped on the side.

Wild Man spun around and stepped out to allow the football players to place Zach in the chair. They showed him how to operate it and moved aside as Zach took two victory laps around the stage. With tears streaming, two thousand students and faculty members simultaneously leaped to their feet to give a five-minute standing ovation.

Were they just cheering for Zach and the fact that he could now remain in their school? No, they were also cheering for Wild Man, who had used his own initiative to rally for Zach's new chair. His mohawked, tattooed, punk-rocker friends had caught wind of his special need and had banded together and collected enough money on their own to buy the chair.

So, it's true: we shouldn't judge a book by its cover. When given a chance to feel wanted, important, capable, and needed, even the most deceiving "books" can deliver a great moral to the story. Remember: "A broken clock is right twice a day." Never give up on anyone!

Commitment

There is a suicide epidemic in the world today. It affects everyone from forty-year-olds going through a midlife crisis to students in our schools. In Plano, Texas, several teenagers killed themselves in the same week. It is happening all over the country: the South Shore of New Jersey; Pine Ridge, South Dakota; Orange County, California; Dade County, Florida; Toronto, Canada. In Iowa, there were one hundred suicide attempts in thirty days at the same high school. One girl died. The school brought Charlotte Ross, a national consultant on suicide, and me in to talk to the kids. We split up the student body into two groups. Charlotte did the left brain, cognitive, therapy presentation. I did the right brain, emotional, motivational presentation. We then swapped audiences and repeated our presentations. Finally, we gathered with counselors and healthcare professionals to interview each of the students who had attempted suicide.

The demographic breakdown of those ninety-nine students was enlightening: 73 percent were on the honor roll. They said, "Thanks for the recognition, but I still have a giant hole in my heart. Something is missing in my life. Please help me!" Six students were student-body officers elected by classmates. They said, "Thanks for letting us win a popularity contest, but I'm missing something in my life." Three students were cheerleaders. They said, "Thanks for the attention, but it's shallow and fleeting." Three students were varsity football players. They said, "We were injured. Our bodies let us down. Because we can't be athletes, we are nobody. There is nothing left."

In a corporate setting, they are the employees of the month. In the community, they are the "good kids." In school, they are the stars with recognition, accolades, and constant attention. So why did they want to give up and take their lives?

Each one told us they lacked "commitment relationships" in their lives. That was the phrase they used, and it caught my attention. To help us define commitment, let us introduce another word: *love*. Love is commitment, not a way of feeling. Romance is not love. Think of it this way: If I love you because you are beautiful, that's romance. But if you are beautiful because I love you, that's real love. It's a value-creating love that inspires us to be the best we can be even when the person we love is away. It makes us honestly say, "I like me best when I'm with you. I want to see you again."

Because of movies and music we say, "I love her sooo much. She makes me feel different than I've ever felt before." Feelings, emotions, and hormones are not enough to sustain a relationship.

As important as the words "I love you" are to our mental health and emotional stability, when it comes to commitment relationships, the words "I need you" are the most powerful words. In the context of love, we should say, "I don't love you because I need you; I need you because I love you." Think about it. As you do, let me validate the deep yet elementary importance of "need."

My friend was getting married. He asked me to write a song and sing it at his wedding. I said no. He answered, "I need you." I couldn't say no again. I wrote the song. Two days later, he phoned me back to explain that the band had just canceled, and he wanted me to prepare forty to fifty songs to play as the dinner entertainment. I emphatically said, "No way!" He said, "I need you." I couldn't say no.

Again, let me pause and validate this discussion before I continue. If, as a stranger, I say, "I love you, come on, let's go," you will interpret it as sexual harassment and say, "Absolutely not." But if I say, "I need you to help me," you react by saying, "Where's the fire? We can put it out. Let's go."

I practiced and prepared my music. My friend's wedding finally arrived. I sang the song I wrote for the couple and sang one of the forty to fifty I had practiced for the dinner. Before I could sing another song, the band arrived. There was a miscommunication. I didn't want to sing all night. I wanted to eat and socialize like everybody else, so I helped the band set up their equipment.

When I arrived at the wedding reception, I arrived with the attitude that my friend needed me. I would have stayed until four o'clock in the morning if necessary because he needed me. I would have waited tables, mopped the floor, and contributed in any way I could. But the second the band showed up, I was no longer needed. In all truth, they could do without me. We can fool others, but we can't fool ourselves. Why hang around if I was no longer needed? I didn't. I left the reception and went home.

This is the message coming through loud and clear from adults and young people across North America, especially from those we interviewed in Iowa who attempted suicide. Each one of them told us they knew they were loved, but they didn't believe they were needed.

In the corporate arena, when sales champions or outstanding executives jump ship to work for the competition, it is not about money. They no longer feel needed where they are, so they go where they do feel needed. The students in Iowa put on a good outward show that all was well. Most of us buy into thinking outside attention and recognition motivates us. It doesn't, yet we emphasize it in our marriages, personal relationships, business contracts, and athletic endeavors. We desperately need to be needed. That's what keeps us motivated and hanging around.

The tough reality is that we can't afford to wait for someone else to tell us or show us that we are needed. It might not ever happen. We could go months before we experience this crucial validation. So what do we do: give up and kill ourselves? Most definitely not. Private victories must precede public victories. Who are we fooling to think it is society's responsibility to give our lives meaning, purpose, and excitement? It is our responsibility to do something on a daily basis to prove to ourselves that we are needed. The solution then is to participate more and be involved. We must reach out and make the move to establish and nurture commitment relationships based on action, participation, and proactively creating symbiotic, desired results.

In a relationship, saying "I need you" is not codependency. Rather, it means "I am okay, but I would be so much more with you. You complete me." At the beginning of the wedding, I felt as if I was not just good, I was good for something. I felt that my little weird-shaped puzzle piece really did fit, that I could make a significant contribution. When the band showed up, I lost that understanding. The way we recapture it in any phase of our lives, especially in our personal and professional relationships, is to change our attitude from "What's in it for me?" to "What's in it for others?" The best way for us to prove to ourselves that we are needed is to go out of our way to lift everybody else's performance up to a higher level when we are around. We could call it the "Michael Jordan factor." Let's face it. We work harder in relationships, in sports, in church, in school, in our communities, and in everyday life when we know we make a special difference to others. Saying "I need you" is telling them how you feel, expressing that without them, there wouldn't be everybody.

Attitude

Attitude

It was the third game of Danny's sophomore year. His University of Utah football team had not yet won a game, and they had just been beaten by more than twenty points by a much-inferior, last-place team. It was the day after the game and Danny's team was assembled in the meeting room watching the game films of the embarrassing loss. Suddenly the coach yelled, "Stop the projector. Run that play again."

To the team, the play was not that impressive. The opposing team's running back got the ball and ran around the end with a Utah player coming up and hitting him hard. The Utah player bounced off their guy who continued to run down the field for an additional twenty-five yards before he was finally tackled from behind. This play impressed the Utah coach so much that he rewound and watched the play seven times in a row. He finally said, "Turn off the projector, turn on the lights, and listen to what I'm about to teach you.

"It appears to me that only one player on our team understands the key to winning success. When our guy Danny came up and hit their guy, it was obvious in the film that Danny bounced off and missed the tackle! But Danny was the same guy who tackled their guy twenty-five yards down the field. Danny wasn't even supposed to play or see any action. He was third string on the depth chart. But when the first two players ahead of him got injured, Danny was put in the game. From now on, Danny will start every game. He is my kind of guy. You see, Danny's attitude is right. And when your attitude is right, your abilities will always catch up!"

Bamboo

Lacking a deeper intellectual and spiritual dimension, mere patience allows the emotional "weather" around us to affect our attitudes and resolve. Sure, we might endure pain for a while, but eventually we become distracted and overwhelmed. The higher awareness of perseverance fortifies us to stay determined, stay on task, and believe that everything will turn out in the end—because if it's not okay, it's not the end!

Do you get frustrated when your valiant efforts on behalf of an initiative at work don't bear the desired fruit? It's tempting to throw up your hands and say, "This is pointless!" Significant people hang in there, not merely because they're always looking for the "point" behind the apparent pointlessness, but because they also realize that any organic growth is unsteady, with the fruits materializing when we least expect them and often in unexpected forms.

When you plant a Chinese bamboo tree, water it, and fertilize it, nothing happens for the first year. There's no sign of growth. The same thing happens—or doesn't happen—the second year. The tree is carefully watered and fertilized each year, but nothing shows for eight years. Suddenly, in the ninth year, it grows thirty-nine inches in twenty-four hours, to reach its full height of ninety-eight feet and as large as eight inches in diameter—in just three to four months.

What would have happened if we'd given up after eight years? We don't have to look hard to find analogies in the business world. Notre Dame University marketing expert Herbert True has found that 44 percent of all sales professionals quit after the first call, 24 percent after the second call, 14 percent after the third call, and 12 percent after the fourth call. This means that 94 percent of all sales professionals quit by the fourth call. Absurd, don't you think, when 60 percent of all sales are made *after* the fourth call? When it comes to the profession of selling, we must remember there is a difference between the sales "process" (which is growing together in the out-of-sight ways of trust, clarity, character, confidence, consistency, cause, and chemistry, knowing that in the beginning there is no specific time frame) and the sales "presentation," when we actually make the appointment to sign the contract and close the deal.

Significance brings glory, to borrow William Barclay's word, but the actual practice of significance is a daily slog, a faithful plodding driven by our love for what we are doing and the cherished dreams that follow from and reflect that love. Major League Hall of Famer Cal Ripken Jr., nicknamed "ironman" because he started and played in 2,632 consecutive games over seventeen seasons, didn't set out to claim this incredible record. He simply worked hard at what he loved every day, every practice, and every game, and the record set itself. He didn't merely show patience—he persevered!

Class

I was flying cross-country on a Boeing 757 jet, sitting in first class.
I always fly first class—not because I pay for the ticket, but because I fly more
than two hundred thousand miles per year on Delta Airlines and am a Platinum
Medallion member (four-million miler) who automatically gets upgraded. There
are twenty-four seats in first class, and I was sitting in my usual window seat.

After about two hours and five diet Cokes into the flight, I got up to use the
lavatory. When I walked in and locked the door, I immediately noticed that the
tiny bathroom was totally trashed. There was water everywhere, soapy slime drip-
ping down the mirror, used paper towels on the floor, and crap on the seat. Then it
hit me. The next person who comes in will immediately think I did all of this! So
I started to clean it. With one hand holding my nose and doing everything I could
not to throw up, I wiped the mirror and the seat, cleaned up the trash, and mopped
up the floor. It was clearly one of the most appalling experiences of my life.

When I had relieved my bladder, I emerged from the lavatory and stood in
front of the entire first-class section until I got eye contact with every person sitting in front of me. I was raised to be a gentleman, so I didn't say anything. But I
wanted so badly to yell, "Okay, which one of you low-budget loser bums did this?"
As I sat down, I realized you cannot buy class. Sitting in first class doesn't make you
first-class! You can lie to others and fake out the world, but you cannot lie to yourself. It truly is what we do when no one is around that defines who we really are.

Elevator Gas

On a more humorous but equally disgusting note, when we landed, I checked into my hotel and went to bed. The next morning, I boarded the elevator on the twentieth floor to go downstairs to the ballroom to speak to thirty-five hundred people attending the general session of a convention. I was on the elevator alone until it stopped on the fifteenth floor. On walked a large man dressed in an expensive suit. As soon as the doors shut, he passed gas in a long, loud, offensive way. I couldn't believe it! He looked sophisticated on the outside, but he lacked couth on the inside!

Then, wouldn't you know it? He got off on the very next floor, leaving just as it started to smell. My eyes were watering and my saliva dried up. I've hit skunks on the road that smelled better. Then, "ding," the elevator doors opened on the tenth floor, and eight people with conference name tags hanging around their necks got on. They were going to be in my audience, and every one of them was staring at me in disgust, thinking I was the skunk.

I wanted to explain and tell them what had happened, but I couldn't. In this case, it's more truth than humor that rank character can linger a long time. There's something to be said about leaving a positive legacy and taking pride in how we will be remembered after we are gone.

Get Yourself Right

A father came home from work one afternoon and his son wanted him to spend some time playing with him. The father knew he had work he had to get done that couldn't wait. The son was very insistent, and the father had to come up with something to keep the young boy occupied.

On the coffee table lay a magazine that contained a map of the world. The father ripped the map into numerous tiny pieces, gave the pieces to his young son, and instructed him to go put the map back together.

The son left the room and the father got to work, thinking it would take a number of hours for the son to put the puzzle together. To his surprise, just fifteen minutes later, the son was back and the puzzle was assembled. Amazed, the father asked how he finished so quickly.

"It was easy. On the other side of the map was a picture of a man. When I got the man right, the whole world was right!"

Time Management

A time management seminar presenter pulled out a one-gallon wide-mouthed jar. Then he produced a dozen fist-sized rocks and carefully placed them one by one into the jar. When the jar was filled to the top and no more rocks would fit inside, he asked, "Is this jar full?"

Everyone in the class said, "Yes."

He then reached under the table and pulled out a bucket of gravel. He dumped some gravel in and shook the jar, causing pieces of gravel to work themselves down into the spaces between the big rocks.

He asked the group again, "Is this jar full?"

"Probably not," they answered.

He then reached under the table and brought out a bucket of sand. He started dumping the sand in the jar, and it went into all the spaces left between the rocks and the gravel.

Once more he asked the question. "Is this jar full?"

"No!" the class shouted.

Then he grabbed a pitcher of water and began to pour it in until the jar was filled to the brim.

He looked at the class and asked, "What is the point of this time management illustration?"

One raised his hand and said, "The point is, no matter how full your schedule is, if you try really hard, you can always fit some more things into it."

"No," the speaker replied, "that's not the point. The truth this illustration teaches us is that if you don't put the big rocks in first, you'll never get them in at all. And the big rocks in your life are your children, your spouse, your friendships, your education, your dreams, a worthy cause, teaching or mentoring others, doing things that you love, taking time for yourself, and your physical and mental health.

"Remember to put these big rocks in first, or you'll never get them in at all. If you sweat the small stuff, then you'll fill your life with worrying about things that don't really matter, and you'll never have the quality time you need to spend on the big rocks, the really important stuff."

Just a Little Extra Effort

Jim McMahon, the great quarterback for the 1985 Super Bowl Champion Chicago Bears, is the epitome of effort. From his days of Pop Warner football through his high school, college, and professional days, every time he walked onto the field he knew he could win—not by accident, fate, or fluke but by extra effort.

It was December 19, 1980, Holiday Bowl III. Jim McMahon's nationally ranked Brigham Young University (BYU) Cougars were playing against the Southern Methodist University (SMU) Mustangs. There were four minutes and seven seconds left to play in the game. SMU was winning, 45–25. BYU called time-out, and Coach LaVell Edwards motioned McMahon to the sideline. Edwards said, "Let's see if we can save a little face and score before the game ends."

McMahon got upset. "Coach, what do you mean? We're not quitting! It's not over until it's over!" McMahon went back onto the field, called the team together, and said, "We're gonna win!" He threw a long pass the very next play—touchdown! BYU recovered the ensuing onside kick and scored again on a one-yard scamper by a running back. BYU kicked off, held SMU for three downs, and then blocked the punt and recovered the ball with thirteen seconds left on the clock. McMahon's first two passes were incomplete, but on the very next play, with three seconds left in the game, McMahon completed a forty-six-yard bomb to Clay Brown in the end zone. Brown leaped high into the air to catch it and the game was tied! Gunther came onto the field and kicked the extra point. BYU won, 46–45.

In 1981 McMahon was runner-up to Marcus Allen for the Heisman Trophy, was the first-round pick by the Chicago Bears, and was named Rookie of the Year.

In 1984 Doug Flutie demonstrated the same dedication and, with his Boston College teammates, won an important game in the same miracle catch manner. Flutie also won the Heisman! These two athletes not only have superior talent, but they also have the superior determination and drive that enables them to make the extra effort that always makes the difference— not just in games, but more important, in practice.

The difference between *good* and *great*, between *winning* and *losing*—between receiving enormous rewards and no rewards at all—is just a little bit of extra effort.

- In 1974 the winning jockey of the Kentucky Derby received $27,000. Less than two seconds later, the jockey who crossed the finish line in fourth place received $30.
- In 1982 Gordon Johncock won the Indianapolis 500 by sixteen hundredths of a second—the length of his car. His paycheck was well over ten times that of the second place finisher, whose name we don't even remember.
- In the 1984 Summer Olympic Games the competitors in the women's long-distance cycling race engaged in a back-and-forth, hard-fought sprint to the finish line. The winner won the race, and thereby the gold medal, by the length of a bicycle wheel.
- In baseball the difference between a .300 hitter who is a millionaire star and a .200 hitter who earns a minimal salary (and finds himself traded from team to team as often as a team manager changes his dirty socks) is one hit in every ten times up to bat. And in those ten times at bat, if both these batters let their batting count go to "full-count" (three balls and two strikes), then the difference between them is only one hit in every sixty pitches!

Sure it's important to have good practice facilities and great coaching—and also some talent to go with it. Sure it's important to believe you are somebody special, equal to the guts and deserving of the glory of McMahon and Flutie. But without that little bit of extra effort, becoming a champion remains only a dream.

In their day, these two athletes not only had superior talent, but they also had the superior determination and drive that enabled them to make the extra effort that always makes the difference— not just in games, but more important, in practice.

There are some people who always give that extra effort. Their inspiration to me is timeless. I could list several more recent examples of athletes who embody this philosophy, but I happen to know these following extraordinary individuals and so I wanted to share their stories with you.

Together We Can Make It

Bob Butler lost his legs in a 1965 land mine explosion in Vietnam. He returned home a war hero. Twenty years later, he proved once again that heroism comes from the heart.

Butler was working in his garage in a small town in Arizona on a hot summer day when he heard a woman's screams coming from a nearby house. He began rolling his wheelchair toward the house, but the dense shrubbery wouldn't allow him access to the back door. So he got out of his chair and started to crawl through the dirt and bushes.

"I had to get there," he said. "It didn't matter how much it hurt." When Butler arrived at the pool, there was a three-year-old girl named Stephanie Hanes lying at the bottom. She had been born without arms and had fallen into the water and couldn't swim. Her mother stood over her baby, screaming frantically. Butler dove to the bottom of the pool and brought little Stephanie up to the deck. Her face was blue, she had no pulse, and she was not breathing.

Butler immediately went to work performing CPR to revive her while Stephanie's mother telephoned the fire department. She was told that the paramedics were already out on a call. Helplessly, she sobbed and hugged Butler's shoulder.

As Butler continued with his CPR, he calmly reassured her. "Don't worry," he said. "I was her arms to get out of the pool. It'll be okay. I am now her lungs. Together we can make it."

Seconds later the little girl coughed, regained consciousness, and began to cry. As they hugged and rejoiced together, the mother asked Butler how he knew it would be okay.

"When my legs were blown off in the war, I was all alone in a field," he told her. "No one was there to help except a little Vietnamese girl. As she struggled to drag me into her village, she whispered in broken English, 'It okay. You can live. I be your legs. Together we make it.'"

He told the mother that this was his chance to return the favor.

See

It was a hot, sunny day, and a man was lounging at the hotel pool. Clad in a bright orange swimsuit and sleek wraparound sunglasses, the man casually sipped a frozen drink. Soon a woman lay down on the chaise to the right of him and commented, "What a drag. There are clouds in the sky, and one of them is going to cover the sun. It's even getting windy."

The man in the sunglasses replied, "No, it's a wonderful day. Can't you see the birds chirping in the trees? Can't you see that the clouds and breeze will cool down the blistering heat?"

In a moment, it started to sprinkle. The woman complained, "What did I tell you? This rain ruins everything."

The man in the sunglasses said, "No, it doesn't. Can't you see that the magnificent, fragrant flowers blossoming all around us and the freshly cut grass need the rain?"

Soon a couple pulled up chairs and sat down to the left of him. "You idiot. I can't believe you locked the key in the room," the man yelled at his wife.

"Yeah, but you forgot to bring the suntan lotion, you big imbecile," she replied.

The man in the sunglasses interrupted, "Can't you see there is another key at the front desk and probably lots of lotion in the gift shop? Can't you see that fighting over shallow things is a waste of precious life?"

A mother sitting two seats away asked her son if he would please pick up a heavy box and take it to the car. He complained, "Oh, Mom, my back hurts, I'm tired, and ouch! I just got something in my eye!"

The man in the sunglasses turned to the lad. "Can't you see there are people in this world who would give anything just to be able to bend over and lift something?"

Just then, a woman came from behind the wall with a wheelchair. She helped hoist the paralyzed, blind man into the seat, rearranged his sunglasses, carefully wheeled him out of the gate, and extended his telescopic white cane so that he could tap his way back to the positive environment of his hotel room.

Losing Your Marbles

The older I get, the more I enjoy Saturday mornings. Perhaps it's the quiet solitude that comes with being the first to rise, or maybe it's the unbounded joy of not having to be at work. Either way, the first few hours of a Saturday morning are most enjoyable.

A few weeks ago, I was shuffling toward the kitchen with a steaming cup of coffee in one hand and the morning paper in the other. What began as a typical Saturday morning turned into one of those lessons that life seems to hand you from time to time. Let me tell you about it.

I turned the volume up on my radio in order to listen to a Saturday morning talk show. I heard an older-sounding chap with a golden voice. You know the kind; he sounded like he should be in the broadcasting business himself.

He was talking about "a thousand marbles" to someone named "Tom." I was intrigued, and sat down to listen to what he had to say. "Well, Tom, it sure sounds like you're busy with your job. I'm sure they pay you well, but it's a shame you have to be away from home and your family so much. Hard to believe a young fellow should have to work sixty of seventy hours a week to make ends meet. Too bad you missed your daughter's dance recital."

He continued, "Let me tell you something, Tom, something that has helped me keep a good perspective on my own priorities." And that's when he began to explain his theory of a "thousand marbles."

"You see, I sat down one day and did a little arithmetic. The average person lives about seventy-five years. I know, some live more and some live less, but on average, folks live about seventy-five years.

"Now then, I multiplied 75 times 52 and I came up with 3,900, which is the number of Saturdays that the average person has in his or her entire lifetime. Now stick with me, Tom. I'm getting to the important part.

"It took me until I was fifty-five years old to think about all this in any detail," he went on, "and by that time, I had lived through more than twenty-eight hundred Saturdays. I got to thinking that if I lived to be seventy-five, I only had about a thousand of them left to enjoy. So I went to a toy store and bought every single marble they had. I ended up having to visit three toy stores to round up a thousand marbles. I took them home and put them inside of a large, clear plastic container right here in my workshop next to the radio.

"Every Saturday since then, I have taken one marble out and thrown it away. I found that by watching the marbles diminish, I focused more on the really important things in life. There is nothing like watching your time here on this earth run out to help get your priorities straight!

"Now let me tell you one last thing before I sign off with you and take my lovely wife out for breakfast. This morning, I took the very last marble out of the container. I figure if I make it until next Saturday, then God has blessed me with a little extra time to be with my loved ones.

"It was nice to talk to you, Tom. I hope you spend more time with your loved ones, and I hope to meet you again someday. Have a good morning!"

You could have heard a pin drop when he finished. Even the show's moderator didn't have anything to say for a few moments. I guess he gave us all a lot to think about. I had planned to do some work that morning and then go to the gym. Instead, I went upstairs and woke my wife with a kiss. "C'mon, honey, I'm taking you and the kids to breakfast."

"What brought this on?" she asked with a smile.

"Oh, nothing special," I said. "It has just been a long time since we spent a Saturday together with the kids. Hey, can we stop at a toy store while we're out? I need to buy some marbles."

May you have many happy years after you lose all your marbles!

Positive Thinking

$2 + 2 = 4$. Whether you think positive or negative, the answer is the same. Right? Not according to George.

When George was in college, jobs were tough to find unless you graduated in the top 5 percent of your class. Therefore, he studied very hard. He had been up all night cramming and went running into class late. He missed the math professor's explanation. He grabbed the test, sat down at his desk, and started the eight problems in front of him. He finished the test with ease and turned it in. The professor said George hadn't even attempted the two extra credit problems he had written on the chalkboard. George pleaded for more time, and the professor let him take the test home. He promised he would turn it in the following morning. He stayed up all night and finally finished one problem. He was depressed because he was out of time, but he turned in the unfinished test as he promised.

The next morning, a knock came at his door. He answered and found his math professor. "George, George, you've made mathematics history!" the professor proclaimed. "You missed my explanation before class that we shouldn't worry if we can't solve all the problems. Some are impossible to solve. Not even Einstein could solve them. I put two of them on the board. George, you solved one of the problems! How did you do it?"

George pondered for a minute and then explained, "If I had heard your explanation that the problems were impossible, do you think I would have even tried to solve them? No way. But with a positive attitude, I attacked the problems and one solution finally came!"

It's true. You can if you think you can!

The Wisdom of Youth

Rebecca sat down and wrote God a personal letter. It read, "Dear God, I've been a good girl, so please send me one hundred dollars so I can buy a bicycle. Love, Rebecca."

When the postman saw the letter addressed to God, he didn't know what to do. So he added an address and sent it on to Washington, D.C. When one of the secretaries at the government agency opened the letter, she was touched by the little girl's request. In response, she immediately put a ten-dollar bill in an envelope, addressed it, and mailed it back to Rebecca.

Rebecca was excited when she received the letter but was puzzled as to why it said "Washington, D.C., Confidential." She quickly opened the envelope and found the ten-dollar bill.

She sat down and wrote a thank-you letter.

"Dear God, You are wonderful! Thank you for the money. But next time, don't send it through Washington. They kept ninety dollars of it!"

In any discussion of government taxation, this story is an amusing anecdote. It illustrates that the methods our government uses to generate revenues don't always seem fair to the working people who pay the bulk of the taxes.

Nevertheless, there are situations in life that are best endured by maintaining a good sense of humor. Everybody wonders where those tax dollars go, and this story illustrates our feelings about the politics of government.

Sometimes it takes the wisdom and observations of a child to help us get a grip on our gripes.

The Power of Imagination

One of the most dramatic stories to come out of the Vietnam War was that of Air Force Colonel George Hall.

While in solitary confinement as a prisoner of war in North Vietnam, George played an imaginary round of golf each day for five and a half years. In his black pajamas and bare feet in his solitary cube, he would put an imaginary golf ball down and hit his drives, straight and true, down the middle of a plush green fairway, perhaps Pebble Beach or Augusta National. For five and a half years, he replayed in his imagination every course he had played before. He replaced every divot, chipped onto the green, blasted balls out of sand traps, and then raked the traps smooth again. He pulled out the flag, got on one knee, and checked the break to see whether the ball would break toward the ocean or down the slope. He putted down the hole, walked on to the next tee, and washed his ball in the ball wash of his imagination.

After all those years in solitary confinement, he was back in form less than a month after his release. Colonel Hall played in the New Orleans Open, paired with Orville Moody, the old pro. The colonel shot a seventy-six!

When it was over, a skeptical reporter stopped him and indignantly asked, "I know you've been locked up in prison and wasted away the last five or six years of your life, so what happened here today?"

The colonel smiled and offered an answer for the ages. "Prison is more a state of mind than it is a physical deprivation. In war, in sports, and in life, we must realize that the body will endure anything. It's the mind we must convince. You cannot always control what happens to you, but you can control how you deal with it. I was tortured and interrogated every day, but I believed Einstein's words that 'imagination is more important than knowledge.' So I practiced golf in my mind."

The journalist challenged him, "If you were under interrogation by the North Vietnamese captors, where did you find the time?"

"Each day, I decided to get up one hour earlier before the guards came. Do this for a year, and you will have added fifteen twenty-four-hour days to your waking world. I did this for five and a half years and it paid off ! It was the secret to my survival and my performance today."

"So, what do I write in my article?"

The colonel replied, "Life is like golf—full of hazards and traps. Focus on the green instead of the sand and get your internal swing right. When your swing is right, golf is right, life is right, and the world is right. Imagination is the most powerful nation on Earth!"

Communication

Art Form

Communication is not just two people taking turns talking. It's an art form where an open line of complete understanding exists. Tragedy lurks amid poor communication.

A mother's three-year-old daughter had opened the front door and walked down the busy street. From her window, the mother could see her little girl standing on the curb as trucks, buses, and cars whizzed by. She raced out toward her daughter, grabbed her, and scolded, "How many times have I told you not to go by the curb?"

Her daughter looked at her innocently and asked, "Mommy, what's a curb?"

Effective communication breeds understanding on an intuitive, spiritual plane that words cannot explain.

My car broke down in the rain late at night on an obscure country road. No one knew I was out there. Within fifteen minutes, my dad pulled up and said, "Hop in. We'll tow it in the morning." He never told me how he knew I was in trouble. Parents mysteriously communicate with their children heart-to-heart, spirit-to-spirit, sometimes without speaking a single word. Dads give good-night kisses and tuck us in bed to officially eliminate fright. Mothers kiss an "ouchie" and somehow magically make it all better.

Communication can always be good, pure, powerful, and positive. It should always be this way. It will always be this way if you want it to be. Choose for it to be and allow it to be!

Everything I Needed to Learn in College, I Learned Outside of Class

In-the-box right answers present a challenge. Too often, the learned discount them because they are simple and ordinary enough for the unlearned to understand. For some reason, we think that unless an answer is complicated, it isn't sophisticated, and if it's obvious, it can't be a life-altering or educational experience worth our while. Apparently they have never met anybody like my big buddy Blain!

He was my first roommate at college. A big, strong, soft-spoken cowboy, he had a huge smile, was always polite, and did not speak much. When we met, I asked, "What's your name?"

"Blain," he answered.

Five minutes of silence later, I asked, "Where are you from?"

"Idaho."

Five minutes of silence later, I asked, "Do you live in the city or the country?"

"Country."

Five minutes of silence later, I asked, "What is your major?"

"Communications."

Yes, Blain was a man of few words, but when he did speak, he was always deep and profound. In our first seven days together, Blain taught me everything I needed to know to succeed for the rest of my life. For the rest of forever, I will always know the answers are definitely in the box.

Day One: We were late checking into our dorm room, so we got last pick of the accommodations. We were told that the only thing left was an older corner room. I complained all the way down the hall, moaning, "I never get a break." Then we opened the door and saw a big, oak-trimmed suite. Blain quietly said, "The early bird gets the worm, but the second mouse always gets the cheese."

Day Two: I had an old car with squeaky brakes. I asked Blain if he knew anything about cars. He said, "I'll see." That afternoon, he jacked up my car and took off a wheel. He quickly checked it and put it back on. He then opened the hood and fiddled around for a minute. Dumbfounded, I asked him what he was doing. He simply replied, "I couldn't fix your brakes, so I just made your horn louder!"

Day Three: We had the first class of the day together. It was Introduction to Marketing. The professor said, "Take thirty minutes and write an ad. Use as many words as necessary, but keep it to one page." After a while, the professor called on three different people to share. They read full-page, wordy essays. The professor then called on Blain. He quietly read, "For sale: Parachute, only used once, never opened, small stain." We laughed. The professor was intrigued and inquired if he had any other thoughts he would like to share. Blain quietly drawled, "Well, I kinda sorta got a real-estate marketing idea I also wrote here."

The professor said, "Yes?" as we all held our breath.

Blain read, "Statistics prove that most people have serious accidents within five miles of their home. So call me as your realtor, and I'll help you move!" We all burst into belly-shaking hoots and cheers.

Day Four: The sociology professor ironically didn't seem to care about anything or anyone. He didn't call the roll and only talked for one minute at the beginning of class to tell us what chapters to read. Then he sat down, put his feet up on a table, and read a magazine for the next thirty minutes. I commented to Blain, "How can he teach us when he is not even involved in the class?"

"He can't," Blain replied. "You can't farm from the city." I then asked him if he were the professor, what would he teach? Blain replied, "Ninety percent of success is half mental."

I laughed and asked, "What?"

With a serious face, Blain explained: "Yep. Success is 10 percent inspiration and 90 percent perspiration. It's 10 percent what happens to you and 90 percent what you do with what happens to you. The half mental is attitude and the other half is action."

Day Five: Already, some of the guys in our dorm had started to party during the week with their wild roommates. I commented, "Mike came in here straight, with high moral standards and high athletic and education goals, but John sure is a bad influence on him."

Blain replied, "Yep. I had to write poetry in English class today and wouldn't you know it, it pretty much explains what's goin' on with these fellas: 'On top of old Smoky all covered with snow, I lost my best bird dog by aiming too low.' It's better to shoot for the stars and miss than to aim for a pile of manure and hit!"

I hadn't seen Blain talk this much all at once since I met him, and I definitely didn't want to cut him off. I'm glad I didn't because he then shared this poem:

> With garbage and junk our big can is well fed,
> This trash we don't want we can burn it instead.
> But what about dirt that you've heard or you've said,
> Oh what can be done with a garbage can head?

Day Six: It was the weekend, and I asked Blain if he wanted to go to a party. We went. Within fifteen minutes, the fraternity boys tried to pressure him with the usual, "C'mon. Chill out. Loosen up. Smoke a little dope, drink a few shots, get down tonight." I asked him if he wanted to leave. Blain answered, "No. But they shouldn't try to teach a pig to sing. It's a waste of your time, and it annoys the pig! Why should I let what others say and do change who I am or what I do?"

Day Seven: I was tired and wanted to sleep in. But Blain was up bright and early. I asked him where he was going all dressed up. He said, "Church."

Sarcastically I poked fun. "Why would you go to church? Your parents aren't here to make you."

Blain put me in my place with his answer: "It's what you do when the coach is not around that makes you a champion. We shouldn't just learn and do things that will help us while we're alive; we should learn and do things that will help us when we're dead! You should come to church with me."

I defiantly demanded, "Give me one good reason why I should."

Blain pretty much summed up the week and the previous in-the-box principles of success he had already taught me when he answered, "It's better to build a fence at the edge of the cliff than to park an ambulance at its base!"

Support

John McMaster became a superstar basketball player in high school. For each of his three years on the team, he was All-Conference, and All-State. In his final season, he was named the Most Valuable Player in the league. John's mother never missed a game at home or away, regardless of the travel distance or weather conditions. She always bought a season pass and was always in the bleachers cheering her son to victory.

Interestingly, John's mother was totally blind. What's the message? Although the mother could not see her son, he could see her. Support makes the special difference!

Milking the Message
Out of Every Moment

One year we had an interschool boxing tournament to raise money for charity. I volunteered to fight a guy and needed a trainer/manager for my corner. I asked a favorite teacher, Coach Ted Weight, to assist me. After round one was finally over, I staggered back to my corner all beaten up and dejected. I sat down on the stool, looked up at Coach Weight for some encouragement, and asked, "Did I hit him at all? Am I doing any damage?"

Coach solemnly replied, "No, but keep swinging. Maybe the draft will give him a cold."

Coach Weight taught me to always do my best, but to keep things in perspective and always have fun while doing it. It was only a boxing match!

The other day, I was at my friend's home, and his tenth-grade son came into the kitchen. With his speech impediment, he told his dad, "I-I-I w-w-wa-want t-t-t-to try out f-f-fo-for the debate team." His dad always supported him and believed in him; his dad told him he thought he could do it. Later that day, the son came home from school, dejected and down. His dad asked him if he made the debate team. His son replied, "N-n- n-no. Th-th-th-they s-s-sa-said I w-w-wa-wasn't tall enough." Obviously this empathetic debate teacher knew that if there is a reason to be negative, we should not focus on things we cannot change, which always keeps the hope alive to improve the things we can change.

A Brother's Song

Like any good mother, when Karen found out that another baby was on the way, she did what she could to help her three-year-old son, Michael, prepare for a new sibling. They found out that the new baby was going to be a girl, and day after day, night after night, Michael sang to his little sister in Mommy's tummy.

He was building a bond of love with his little sister before he even met her. The pregnancy progressed normally for Karen and in time, the labor pains came. But serious complications arose during delivery and Karen found herself in hours of labor. Finally, after a long struggle, Michael's little sister was born. She was in very serious condition. The ambulance rushed the infant to the neonatal intensive care unit at St. Mary's Hospital in Knoxville, Tennessee. The days inched by. The little girl got worse. The pediatric specialist regretfully had to tell the parents, "There is very little hope. Be prepared for the worst."

Karen and her husband contacted a local cemetery about a burial plot. They had fixed up a special room in their home for the new baby, but now they found themselves having to plan for a funeral.

Michael, however, kept begging his parents to let him see his sister. "I want to sing to her," he kept saying. Week two in intensive care looked as if a funeral would come before the week was over. Michael kept nagging about singing to his sister, but kids are never allowed in the intensive care unit. Karen made up her mind, though. She would take Michael whether they liked it or not! If he didn't see his sister right then, he may never see her alive.

She dressed him in an oversized scrub suit and marched him into ICU. He looked like a walking laundry basket, but the head nurse recognized him as a child and bellowed, "Get that kid out of here now! No children are allowed!" The mother rose up strong in Karen, and the usually mild-mannered woman glared steel-eyed right into the head nurse's face, her lips a firm line. "He is not leaving until he sings to his sister!"

Karen towed Michael to his sister's bedside. He gazed at the tiny infant losing the battle to live. After a moment, he began to sing. In the pure-hearted voice of a three-year-old, Michael sang: "You are my sunshine, my only sunshine, you make me happy when skies are gray." Instantly, the baby girl seemed to respond. Her pulse rate began to calm down and become steady. "Keep on singing, Michael," encouraged Karen with tears in her eyes.

"You'll never know, dear, how much I love you. Please don't take my sunshine away."

As Michael sang to his sister, the baby's ragged, strained breathing became as smooth as a kitten's purr. "Keep on singing, sweetheart!"

"The other night, dear, as I lay sleeping, I dreamed I held you in my arms . . ." Michael's little sister began to relax and rest, a healing rest that seemed to sweep over her.

"Keep on singing, Michael." Tears had now conquered the face of the bossy head nurse. Karen glowed.

"You are my sunshine, my only sunshine. Please don't take my sunshine away. . ."

The next day . . . the very next day . . . the little girl was well enough to go home!

Woman's Day magazine called it "The Miracle of a Brother's Song." The medical staff just called it a miracle. Karen called it a miracle of God's love! To the world, you may be one person, but to one person, you may be the world.

Positive Discipline

I was recently visiting with Mr. Croft, one of my former high school teachers. We were discussing mutual respect and support in the context of positive discipline. I was looking for a firsthand experience from the world of education that would apply to parenting, coaching, and the corporate world of management, sales, and customer service. The conversation centered on how to motivate, inspire, and empower others—not only to increase performance and productivity, but to keep the rules and show respect.

Mr. Croft asked for my definitions.

With regard to mutual respect and support, I said, "The only place from which a person can grow is where he or she is."

For positive discipline, I said, "You cannot increase a person's performance by making him or her feel worse; humiliation immobilizes behavior."

Mr. Croft's eyes lit up with excitement as he shared the following experience to illustrate his point.

"I had a student who disrupted everything," he said.

"Did you send him to the office?" I asked.

With an offended look on his face, he said, "I've taught school for more than twenty-five years, and I've never sent a student to the principal." Mr. Croft laughed. "Most of my colleagues think the principal has all the Band-Aids. No way. Teachers are responsible for their classrooms and the development and education of each kid. You don't just throw them out when they do something wrong. We have to invite them to grow. We must catch them doing something right."

"Mr. Croft," I interrupted, "I've been to schools where a long line of students trails out the principal's office, down the hall, out the door, and past the 9A bus stop. They're suntanned! And they just stand there with that look of 'Yep, I put a goldfish into the pencil sharpener four months ago, and I'm still waiting to see the principal.' If this is education, we're fooling ourselves! So what did you do with your student?" I asked.

"Interesting you should ask," he replied. "I didn't give up on him. My research uncovered that this James character played in a rock-and-roll band and that he was playing that Friday night in a smoke-filled, honky-tonk, redneck biker bar out in the bushes somewhere. I talked five teachers into going with me so I wouldn't be stabbed all by myself."

"Then what happened?" I asked expectantly.

"Now picture this," Mr. Croft continued. "Six of us in argyle sweaters with matching socks stood at the back of the dance floor surrounded by teenagers who looked like they'd been mugged with a staple gun. The lead singer had a carburetor stuck in his nose. When James spotted us, he leaned into the microphone and asked, 'What are you proctologist-looking teachers doing here?' We told him we heard his band was awesome and wanted to check them out."

Mr. Croft and his colleagues only stayed fifteen minutes. That's all the noise they could take. That was Friday night. On Monday morning, was James a discipline problem in Mr. Croft's class? No way. Was he a problem in Mr. Croft's class the rest of the school year? No way! Was James a discipline problem in other teachers' classrooms for the rest of the school year? Yes! Was it because they couldn't teach? No. It was simply because they didn't care.

Tree Talk

The heroine of this story is an eight-year-old girl in a Pennsylvania orphanage. She was painfully shy and had such annoying mannerisms that she was shunned by the other children and regarded as a problem child by the teachers. Two other orphanages had managed to have her transferred. Now, once again, the director was seeking some pretext for getting rid of her.

One afternoon, it appeared that an opportunity had arrived. An ironclad rule held that any letter from a child in the institution had to be approved by the director or a house mistress before it could be mailed. The little girl had been observed sneaking down to the main gate and carefully securing a letter in the branches of a tree that overhung the wall of the orphanage. The director could scarcely conceal her delight.

She hurried down to the brick wall. Sure enough, the note was visible through the branches of the tree.

The director took it and tore open the envelope. She pulled out the note and quickly read it. Stunned, she stood staring at the paper with tears in her eyes, shame in her heart, and a promise to be a better person. It read: "To anybody who finds this—I love you."

Letter from Camp

Dear Mom,

Our scoutmaster told us all to write to our parents in case you saw the flood on TV and worried. We are okay. Only one of our tents and two sleeping bags got washed away. Luckily, none of us got drowned because we were all up on the mountain looking for Chad when it happened.

Oh yes, please call Chad's mother and tell her he is okay. He can't write because of the cast. I got to ride in one of the search-and-rescue jeeps. It was neat. We never would have found him in the dark if it hadn't been for the lightning. Scoutmaster Webb got mad at Chad for going on a hike alone without telling anyone. Chad said he did tell him, but it was during the fire so he probably didn't hear him. Did you know that if you put a gas can on a fire, it will blow up? The wet wood still didn't burn, but one of our tents did, also some of our clothes. John is going to look weird until his hair grows back. We will be home on Saturday if Scoutmaster Webb gets the car fixed. It wasn't his fault about the wreck. The brakes worked okay when we left. Scoutmaster Webb said that with a car that old you have to expect something to break down; that's probably why he can't get insurance on it. We think it's a neat car. He doesn't care if we get it dirty, and if it's hot, sometimes he lets us ride on the tailgate, and it gets pretty hot with ten people in a car. He let us take turns riding in the trailer until the highway patrolman stopped and talked to us. Scoutmaster Webb is a neat guy. Don't worry, he is a good driver. In fact, he is teaching Terry how to drive. But he only lets him drive on the mountain roads where there isn't any traffic. All we ever see up there are logging trucks.

This morning, all of the guys were diving off the rocks and swimming out in the lake. Scoutmaster Webb wouldn't let me because I can't swim and Chad was afraid he would sink because of his cast, so he let us take the canoe across the lake. It was great. You can still see some of the trees under the water from the flood. Scoutmaster Webb isn't crabby like some scoutmasters. He didn't even get mad about the life jackets. He has to spend a lot of time working on the car, so we are trying not to cause him any trouble.

Guess what? We have all passed our first aid merit badges. When Dave dove in the lake and cut his arm, we got to see how a tourniquet works. Also, Wade and I threw up. Scoutmaster Webb said it probably was just food poisoning from the leftover chicken. He said they got sick that way with the food they ate in prison.

I have to go now. Don't worry about anything. We are fine.

Love,
Cole

Bird Talk

Have you ever tried to teach a bird to talk? I bought a parakeet and promptly started the process. I looked the bird in the eye and said, "Danny, Danny," over and over again. Fifty repetitions a day for two straight months! Three thousand repetitions. Then it finally happened. One morning as I was leaving the room, the parakeet blurted out, "Danny."

Now it was time to teach him his last name, Clark. I followed the same process: "Clark, Clark." It only took two hundred repetitions over a week, and the bird finally said, "Clark." The learning process curve was speeding up!

Then something very interesting happened. I got sick and spent two days in the house coughing and coughing. That weekend, I had a party. When I showed off my talking bird, I discovered a great principle about why we do the things we do. Positive or negative, we learned it all the same way. I got the bird's attention and it said "Danny Clark. Cough!" Yes, the bird coughed.

Now, did I teach the bird to cough? No! The bird was a product of its environment, and so are human beings. What goes into our minds stays and will eventually come back out. How did we learn to talk and walk and sing and dance?

We are not born—we are made. With the right input, we can actually become the "bird" we dream to be!

Interpretation

Let us review a typical family situation where the parent is discussing the touchy subject of curfew with a teenager. Because communication is based on interpretation and understanding of how it looks and feels different to each participant, let us stage this scenario with the parent looking at the teenager with a wall between them. One side of the wall is painted white. The other side is painted blue. The wall represents curfew, and each individual can see only his side and color of the wall.

When the sixteen-year-old teenage daughter is asked, "What color is the wall?" she obviously answers, "White." When the father is asked the same question, he obviously answers, "Blue." Who is right? They both are, depending on their individual perspectives and interpretations.

Dad: "Your curfew is midnight. What good, clean, pure, powerful, positive thing can a teenager do after midnight that will enhance your life and help make your dreams come true? I wasn't born yesterday. The sex monster comes out at midnight. Don't argue with me!"

Daughter: "You are so old-fashioned. Don't you remember what it was like to be a teenager back in the dark ages? I can't help it if you were a cheerleader for Ben Hur! Why do you want me home by midnight? My friends get to stay out until Saturday!"

Dad: "That's it! Don't talk back to me! See, you don't respect me, and therefore, you can't respect yourself, and you'll get into mischief and probably break the law! I brought you into this world; I can take you out of it. You are now grounded! And by the way, I don't approve of some of your friends. You can't hang out with them anymore! If you don't grow up, you will never date until you are thirty years old. Go to your room!"

Daughter: "No! I am leaving. I'm divorcing you as my parent. I'm running away from home to live with my friends in a loving commune where we can do whatever we want. Good-bye!"

Dad: "Good-bye, my eye! Go to your room!

Daughter: "Why should I?"

Dad: "Because I said so!"

What happened here? First of all, the dad is oblivious to the fundamentals of communication. The conversation quickly deteriorated into an egotistical tug-of-war about who is right. Well . . . who is right? They both are, depending on which side of the wall they are on. The daughter sees and knows the wall is white. The dad sees and knows the wall is blue. They are both correct.

The second reason this conversation about curfew got out of hand is that the dad is oblivious to the fundamentals of motivation. No one can motivate anyone. We can only inspire each other to want to motivate ourselves. Motivation, achievement, and high expectations for accomplishment all come from within. It's what they do when their parents are not around that makes or breaks children and makes them champion children. It's what the teenagers do when the coach and teacher are not around that makes them champion athletes or students. Motivation must be example-setting inspiration, which must be turned into empowerment (answering and knowing "why"). Only when we answer "why" can our teenagers act on their own, be responsible when we are not around, and do the right thing simply because it's the right thing to do.

The third thing dear old Dad did that is unacceptable was trying to change his daughter's friends. When parents try to choose their children's friends, they force them to have two sets of friends—those they really hang out with and those they bring home for Mom and Dad's approval. No wonder so many parents don't know their children are involved in drugs, go to wild parties, or are members of a violent street gang. The parents are forcing their children to live two separate lives.

Don't misinterpret my message here. Parents have a right and a responsibility to get to know their children's "real" friends. The influence of associates is extremely important in establishing or changing behavior. When you put a hard-to-catch horse in the same field with an easy-to-catch horse, you usually end up with two hard-to-catch horses. When you put a sick child in the same room with a healthy child, you usually end up with two sick children. Moral of the story? To be great, you have to hang out with the great ones. Parents' challenges and concerns of dealing with their children's friends are legitimate. However, there is only one real challenge. It all boils down to effective communication.

When there are challenges between people, we seldom have a generation gap or a management or labor gap, or even a gap in respect. It is usually a communication gap. In this family scenario, the relationship between dad and daughter was being ripped apart because of a failure to communicate when setting the highest expectation for trusting behavior. This really wasn't about curfew. Curfew was just a boundary similar to the sideline on a football field or a "traveling" rule limiting the number of steps you can take while holding the ball in a basketball game. The idea is to stay in-bounds, play by the rules, and do the right thing. To keep the referees (our parents, teachers, coaches, and preachers) off our back, we need only do the right thing.

How could this family breakup have been avoided? In business, school, sports, and family life, how can we more effectively communicate, set high expectations together, and jointly decide upon a shared vision to establish trusting behavior? The answer is simple. We learn to communicate more effectively by putting less emphasis on who's right and more emphasis on what's right. Remember, we duplicate that which is emphasized and rewarded. Our performance efficiency actually doubles when we are monitored, measured, held accountable, and required to report back.

How is all of this accomplished? The person in authority (in this case, the dad) must make the first move and come around to the other person's side of the issue. The authority figure needs to walk a mile in the other person's shoes and see the world through her glasses. This is the only way to establish trust—the beginning of real communication. Remember, the daughter is absolutely right when she says her wall is white. Then, to complete this process of trust and understanding (reaching out through mutual respect and support), the person in authority needs to open the lines of communication further by inviting the subordinate (child, employee, student, athlete) to now come over to their side. As we team up from each other's side of the issue, we create a safe and civil environment for dialogue, respect individuality, accept consequences for behavior, feel responsible for individual destiny, and feel empowered to do the right thing—not based on who's right, older, bigger, stronger, or more powerful, but based on what's right.

Let us rewind to the family curfew model and replay it with effective communication. First, the dad comes around to his sixteen-year-old daughter's side of the wall, thus removing the issue barrier from between them and placing it in front of them. No longer are they going head-to-head, but rather shoulder-to-shoulder, jointly working together to find the best solution. As the dad is now on his daughter's side, he says that the wall *is* white just like she said. The dad then puts his arms around his daughter, opens his heart and mind, and says, "Daughter, help me see and understand what it is like to be a teenager today from your perspective. Why do you have to stay out so late?"

"Oh, Dad, if I come home at midnight before everybody else, they will think I'm Mama's little lambie pie."

"But what productive things can teenagers do after midnight that will keep you out of trouble and help make your dreams come true? Bars and clubs are closing, and there are more drunk drivers on the road than at any other time. I love you and just want you to come home safe to me."

"Oh, Dad, don't be silly! We're not out on the road. Besides, we like to rent videos and pop popcorn and hang out. We're safely inside of somebody's home."

"Why can't you start the parties earlier?"

"Oh, Dad, we also love to dance at our parties, and the guys are so ugly we have to wait until it gets real dark before we start the music and want to dance with any of them!"

Suddenly, Dad lightens up. "No kidding? That was the same problem we had when I was your age!"

Bursting into laughter, the daughter adds, "Are you joking me? You mean you were actually a teenager once? Are you really starting to understand me? Maybe you're not such an old-fashioned, hard-headed, bad guy after all. Who would have thought you knew so much. And to think you learned it all in just one night!"

The curfew model now continues with the psychological reciprocity, "what-goes-around-comes-around" part. The child is now feeling respect and support. She puts her arms around her dad, opens her heart and mind, and accepts his invitation to gently come over to her dad's side of the wall where she realizes that the color is blue. The admission comes when her dad humorously asks her to honestly answer the question, "If you had you for a child, would you be nervous? Would you want to know who you were with, where you were going, and what reasonable time you would be arriving back home? Now that you have put yourself in my situation, would you have a right and a desire to know if there would be alcohol, drugs, gangs, or drunk driving involved in the evening?"

Accidents are not supposed to happen, but they do because of poor judgment, negligence, and irresponsible parents who are not there with just enough rules, curfew, and regulations to help keep their precious children far enough away from the fire so they don't get burned.

I don't know about you, but if I had me for a child, I wouldn't have even let me go out. I would have been a nervous wreck! I probably would have grounded myself from the time I was three! Let's face it. Parents know a lot more than their children think they know. When I was growing up, my dad told my sister she could not go out with any guy who drove a van. One night a guy drove up, my dad looked out the window, saw the van, and yelled, "Debbie, you can't go out with him. He's driving a van!"

My mother said, "Why? You used to drive a van."

My dad blurted, "That's what I mean. You cannot go out with a guy who drives a van!"

Two-way, open communication is the key to effective teaching, parenting, and coaching. Any group of people can take turns talking. Any educator, parent, or coach can lecture, but it takes a special human being to patiently and lovingly understand and engage in verbal and nonverbal, heart-to-heart, soul-to-soul communication.

Homeless Preacher

One Sunday morning, a homeless man in ragged clothes, carrying a worn-out Bible, entered an upscale church in an exclusive neighborhood. As the man took a seat, those near him moved away. No one greeted or welcomed him.

The preacher approached him and suggested that he ask God what he should wear to church before he came back.

The next Sunday, he showed up again for the services wearing the same ragged clothes and once again was completely shunned and ignored. The preacher approached the man at the end of his sermon and said, "I thought I told you to ask God what the proper attire should be for worshipping in here."

"I did," replied the homeless man, "and God told me that He didn't have a clue what I should wear. He said He'd never been in this church before and said if this was Christianity, He is not a Christian!"

Ethical Forgiveness

A strict disciplinarian stood in front of our class with a crew-cut hairstyle and piercing eyes. He had been a marine drill sergeant in the Vietnam War, had his master's degree in psychology, and was welcoming us as the professor of Business Ethics. Rumor had it that this macho man tolerated nothing. He explained as part of the course orientation that he could always tell if someone cheated. Sarcastically, he illustrated, "One time I called a young man on the carpet. I accused him of cheating. He promised, 'No, I didn't.' I countered, 'Yes, you did.' 'No, I didn't.' 'Yes, you did.' 'How did you know?' he finally confessed. I answered him, 'The young lady you were sitting next to wrote on her test paper, "Don't know the answer." You wrote, 'Me neither!'"

We all laughed at his story, but took it to mean that if anyone got caught cheating, he would "rip their lips off" and flunk them out of school.

The weeks passed uneventfully until the day of the midterm. A guy on the third row was caught cheating. Everyone held their breath as he was asked to leave and turn his exam in early. Surely he would be kicked out of the university. To our surprise, the young man was back in class the next Monday. One indignant student finally raised his hand to interrupt the lecture. "Mr. Jacobsen, Professor, sir. I think this is totally absurd. Here you are teaching a class on ethics. You catch a student red-handed, cheating, and you don't suspend him. What kind of a lesson are you teaching us?"

The professor smiled and replied, "Great question, and I'll answer it with a story."

He told the class the story of a certain one-room schoolhouse in the mountains of California that no teacher could handle. It was a school just for boys so rough that the teachers would resign after only a few short days. A young, inexperienced teacher applied, and the old director warned him about the out-of-control, disrespectful students. The teacher took the job anyway.

On the first day of school the new teacher greeted them, "Good morning, boys. I'm here because I care about you." They yelled, "Yeah, right. You don't even know us," and they laughed and made fun at the top of their voices. The teacher continued, "Now I want a good school, but I confess that I do not know how unless you help me. The things we help create, we support. Suppose we have a few rules. You tell me and I'll write them on the chalkboard."

One fellow yelled, "No stealing." Another yelled, "On time." Finally, ten rules appeared.

"Now," said the teacher, "a law is not good unless there is a consequence attached. What shall we do with one who breaks them?"

Big Jake yelled out, "Beat him across the back ten times without his coat on."

"That is pretty severe, boys. Are you sure that you are ready to stand by it?" They all yelled, "Yeah, yeah, beat them to death," and the teacher said, "Alright, we will live by them. Class, come to order."

Two weeks later, Big Jake, the toughest of the tough, found that his lunch had been stolen. Upon inquiry, the thief was located—a little hungry fellow, ten years old. "We have found the thief and he must be punished according to your rule—ten stripes across the back. Vincent, come up here," the teacher ordered.

The frail little boy, trembling, came up slowly with a big coat fastened up to his neck and pleaded, "Teacher, you can lick me as hard as you like, but please, don't take my coat off."

"Take the coat off," the teacher reminded. "You helped make the rules." As he began to unbutton, the little guy had no shirt on and revealed his bony little crippled body. *How can I whip this child?* the teacher thought. *But I must do what I say I will do if I'm going to keep control and respect of the others.* "How come you are not wearing a shirt, Vincent?" the teacher asked.

"My father died and my mother is very poor," he replied. "I have only one shirt to my name, and she is washing it today, and I wore my brother's big coat to keep me warm."

The teacher, with rod in hand, hesitated and then reluctantly asked Vincent to turn around. Just then Big Jake jumped to his feet and interrupted, "Teacher, if you don't object, I will take Vincent's whipping for him." Hiding his disbelief, the teacher thought quickly on his feet, "Very well, there is a certain law that one can become a substitute for another."

Off came Big Jake's coat, and after five hard strokes, the rod broke. The teacher bowed his head in his hands and thought, *How can I finish this awful task?* Then he heard the class of macho men sniffling and sobbing. What did he see when he lifted his head? Little Vincent had reached up and caught Big Jake with both arms around his neck. "Jake, I'm sorry I stole your lunch, but it had been two days since I had anything to eat. I was extra hungrier than usual. It was just sitting there with no one around and I didn't think. Jake, I will love you until I die for taking my beating for me. I will never steal again. Yes, you are my hero!"

The college professor stopped talking. There wasn't a dry eye in the room. With tears streaming down his cheeks, he said to our class, "My name is Vincent Jacobsen. I was that frail, crippled, hungry lad. We all will make mistakes at some point in our lives, and sometimes all we need is just one break to get our lives back on track. This course is on ethics, and if you remember nothing else, remember that forgiveness is a powerful part of ethical behavior. God bless Big Jake, wherever you are."

Life Lessons

Mall Memories

When I looked beyond the obvious experience of going to the local shopping mall, I learned three significant lessons on successful living.

One

I had borrowed my neighbor's truck to pick up a large package. On the way to the mall, the truck stalled twice. When I arrived at the mall parking lot, it stopped again; this time I could not restart it. Concerned that I had broken my friend's truck, I walked to a repair shop and brought the mechanic back to take a look. He lifted the hood, fiddled around for a few minutes, poured a few drops of fuel into the carburetor, hooked up the jumper cables, and immediately started the engine.

"What's the problem? I asked.

His reply knocked me over. "You are out of gas."

I paid him fifty dollars for the road call and laughed. I learned that attitude is everything. We can own a brand-new car or truck, but unless we motivate it by putting gas in the tank, it can't take us anywhere.

Two

I learned the second lesson inside the mall.

A mother with three small children was approaching the down escalator. Her eight-year-old son inadvertently stepped on the moving step before the rest of the family. Halfway down, he turned around. At the same moment, his mother realized he had slipped away.

"Come back up here right now!" she yelled.

With wide eyes and a determined look on his face, the little lad began sprinting up the moving escalator. A group of us started cheering, "C'mon, Johnny, you can do it!"

The little guy climbed and puffed and climbed some more. But he was going against the tide. One step from the top, he ran out of gas, just like the truck. Too exhausted to continue, he stopped and let the escalator whisk him back to the bottom.

Life is the same way.

It's a fast-moving escalator that never stops. If we want to stay competitive and eventually reach the goals we set in our professional and personal lives, we must keep climbing just like Johnny. But unlike that little lad, we can't stop—or we'll end up back at the bottom!

Three

The third lesson I learned at the mall was a combination of the other two.

We need motivation—fuel in our tanks—but it must be high-octane product motivation, if we expect to get the desired results.

What do you fill up with?

It was Saturday morning at the mall. An expensive sedan stopped near the doorway, and a teenager got out. His mother yelled from inside the car, "I'll pick you up at 7:30 tonight. Stay out of trouble."

For eight hours, the mall was designated as this teen's babysitter. His pals arrived, and they formed small groups, wandering through the mall, amusing themselves by getting in the way of shoppers, making fun of senior citizens, and knocking over trash cans.

For too many teenagers, cruising the mall is the leisure-time activity of choice. When these kids do get in trouble, they make excuses and tell the police that no harm has been done. Sadly, the parents of these youngsters usually don't care. Such parents think their own interests are more important than the mall merchants. Do they understand that we reap only what we sow—input equals output, garbage in, garbage out?

Troublesome youngsters wandering through shopping malls are the product of irresponsible parents. Do you leave your children wandering for hours unsupervised?

Is that the kind of quality time you want your offspring to put in their tank? What is the input? What is the end result? I guarantee that they will run out of gas and quit before they make it to the top.

If you look beyond the obvious, isn't it interesting what one can learn at a mall?

Halftime Score

In our highly competitive world, we must understand that there is nothing more insignificant than the halftime score.

When I was attending the University of Utah, I played football. The game against UCLA was one of our biggest games of the season. Prior to the game, our coach pepped us up, "UCLA doesn't have to win this game. You can if you think you can. Just believe in yourselves. We can win!"

The game started. We got the ball first. They quickly took it away from us. It was our turn to stop them. The guy in front of me was so big I had to look through his legs to see what was going on. He could have kick-started a 747 jet! When they hiked the ball, he hit me so hard that he knocked my helmet around my head so that I was looking out my ear hole. As I stood there crying, I realized my coach was wrong. *UCLA does have to win and I quit,* I thought to myself as I started to walk off the field. The coach wouldn't let me quit. He pushed me back into the huddle. The next play we sacked the quarterback. *I* did! I have to admit that I ran into him by accident, but I still tackled him for a loss. He fumbled the ball. We recovered. We scored. We stopped them and scored twice more. At halftime, the score was 19–0 in favor of the University of Utah. During the first half, UCLA's quarterback thought he was caught in one of those revolving doors at the mall! We lost the game, 23–19.

On another occasion, we played the University of Oklahoma. We were ahead, 7–0. Yes, we were whopping them. It was those last fifty-nine minutes that killed us. We lost, 63–7.

In another game, against the University of Arizona, we were behind at halftime, 21–0. By the end of the third quarter, we were losing 27–0. However, this time we won. We scored our winning points during the last seconds of the game to win 28–27!

We also beat Jim McMahon's BYU team. We were losing at halftime but came from behind to win on a last-second pass. The final score was 23–22. What is the point behind all these games?

Teams that are ahead at halftime are faced with a decision. Either they keep fighting and playing to win, or they stop taking risks and try to live off their past successes by playing "not-to-lose." We play "not-to- lose" when we stop our aggressive offense and replace it with defensive carefulness, when we lose that "eye-of-the-tiger" intensity that gave us the competitive advantage in the first place, when our fear of risk and failure outweighs our desire to succeed.

To win, we must focus and finish. Focusing to W-I-N represents What's Important Now. Then we finish each play from "hello" to "good-bye," one play at a time, until we finish the game. I guess our coaches and parents were right when they taught us, "If it's worth starting, it's worth finishing, because anything worth doing is worth doing right!"

Piano Perfection

When Ernest Saunders was a sixteen-year-old high school student in Philadelphia, he was taken by his music teacher to a scholarship audition at the world-famous Settlement Music School. He took his place at the piano and began to play a complicated concerto. Suddenly, Mrs. Evans, the school official, stood up and applauded and awarded Ernest a full scholarship. He was to enroll immediately. Mrs. Evans was astounded at his ability and said his talent and playing grace were truly magnificent. With tears streaming down her cheeks, Mrs. Evans rushed forward to finish seeing and hearing Ernest brilliantly play the classical piece. Why? He was born with only one finger on his right hand.

Ernest has gone on to record several critically acclaimed albums and is one of the great entertainers, teachers, and modern composers of our time. How? Why? Each day, his students see a Bernard Edmonds quote hanging above his desk that answers all inquiries: "To dream anything that you want to dream. That is the beauty of the human mind. To do anything that you want to do. That is the strength of the human will. To trust yourself to test your limits. That is the courage to succeed!"

A Freshman's First Letter Home

Dear Mom,

I'm sorry it's taken me so long to write. I've never been to the city before. It's my first time away from you, and I'm trying to figure everything out. I don't live where I did when you dropped me off. I read in the paper where most accidents happen within twenty miles of where you live, so I moved.

This place had what I thought was a washing machine. The first day I put four shirts in it, I pulled the chain and haven't seen them since. I finally found the real machine and bought laundry detergent. It said, "ALL," so I dumped the whole box in. I now owe three thousand dollars for water flood damage, but they deducted three hundred dollars because the carpets on all three floors of the dorms are clean!

It only rained twice this week—three days the first time and four days the second time.

The president of my fraternity fell in a whiskey vat at our last party. Some students tried to pull him out, but he fought them off gallantly and drowned. We cremated him but couldn't get the flame to go out. He burned for five days.

Three of my other friends went off a bridge in a pickup. One was driving. The other two were in the back. The driver got out. He rolled down the window and swam to safety. The other two drowned because they couldn't get the tailgate down.

Sincerely,
Your Loving Son

P. S. I was going to send you the expense receipts you requested, but I already had this letter sealed.

The Way It Was and Still Should Be

A special lady lived on a farm in Grace, Idaho. With every challenge or endeavor that came her way, she went far beyond the call of duty. She was a widow with nine children—the youngest age seven, the oldest twenty-two. Instead of complaining of her hard life, she accepted her fate and changed the ordinary into the extraordinary.

No matter how bleak or serious things seemed to be, she found the positive side and a ray of hope. She taught her family the value of hard work and the importance of education, although she only went as far as fourth grade.

Once a week, she picked up supplies in town. Otherwise her days were full milking the cows; making butter, cottage cheese, and ice cream; and raising pigs, sheep, and chickens. She had a large vegetable garden, gooseberry and raspberry bushes, strawberry patches, and apple trees. She was an excellent cook, and neighbors often dropped in at mealtime.

Once when unexpected company arrived, she took her .22 rifle and went outside to shoot a chicken. As the gun went off, another chicken stepped in the line of fire. The bullet went through both chickens and grazed the back of a pig. It became a family joke—one shot to kill two chickens and skin the pig.

Her children didn't have material wealth, but they certainly received the necessary and important things in life: love, spiritual guidance, concern for others, appreciation for a table filled with food, and respect for the law. She was truly an example of all that is good.

I remember as a young man sitting at her feet while she taught me. "If you can't say something nice, don't say anything at all." And, "I'll never throw upon the floor a crust I cannot eat, for many a little hungry one would think it quite a treat. Willful waste brings willful want, and I may live to say, 'Oh, I wish I had that crust that once I threw away.'"

This incredibly strong and courageous woman is my maternal grandmother, Alice Maughan. My mother is a lot like her mother. Many times, my mother went without a new dress just so we could buy some great football cleats for me. Many times, my mother insisted that we stay home instead of going on a summer vacation, just so I could stay and play on a baseball all-star team. My mother is the greatest cook on Earth, a spiritual giant, a church and community servant, and the very best mom who ever lived. She taught me right from wrong and, as far as I know, has never told a lie. I've never heard her swear or complain about her trials, heartache, and pain. My dear, sweet mother, Ruby Maughan Clark, truly is the epitome of service above self. It's the way it was and still should be.

The Spanish Lesson

A wealthy couple, wearing their finest and most expensive clothes and jewels, arrived at a resort in Mexico. The man headed to the golf course to play a round with his buddies. The woman had an invitation to an exclusive auction held only one day each year, one that was sure to have the estate antiques she was looking for.

She hailed a taxi to take her to the auction house. On the way, the driver lost control of the car and slammed into a horse-drawn cart. Animals and produce flew everywhere. Two ten-year-old boys were thrown from the cart into the bushes.

Even though the woman had hurt her head, she scampered to see if they were all right. She found them dazed and bleeding. They pulled back in fright as she came close.

To gain their trust, she pulled out a photograph of her with her four small children. As they inched closer to see, one of the boys asked in broken English, "You mommy?"

She smiled. "Yes, me mommy."

They immediately snuggled in on her lap and hugged her until they stopped shaking. She noticed that one was bleeding from a deep wound on his leg. Since there was no cloth around, she ripped a piece of her dress to bind the gash.

The taxi was demolished, and the driver went to get help. While they were waiting, an old jalopy pulled up. The driver said he would take them to safety—if she paid. "Gladly," she said. But the boys didn't want to leave the produce. They were on their way to sell it at the market, and if they arrived at home empty-handed, they would be in trouble. The woman gave them each twenty-five dollars, which was much more than what they would have made at the market.

When they arrived at the hospital, they could not be admitted until she paid, which she did.

Two hours later, she faced the dilemma of getting the boys back home. Not wanting to risk another cab ride, she called for a limousine.

Delighted with their luck, the boys climbed in and began jabbering in Spanish. The woman didn't understand a word, but she enjoyed their enthusiasm. Along the way, they told the driver to stop. They stepped out and helped a little girl right her fallen wagon. They invited her and her two little girlfriends in for a ride. The five of them talked nonstop.

Before they reached the village, the boys had the driver stop a few more times to pick up more little girls. And when they finally arrived, the boys had a carful.

The children scampered out and disappeared. But before the woman could leave, they all reappeared, each with ice-cream cones.

"Why have the boys spent their precious money buying ice cream for all these strangers?" the woman asked the driver. "And why are they being especially nice to the young girls?"

The driver inquired of the boys. Hugging the woman tightly, they proudly answered, "*Tenemos que cuidaries a ellas especialmente, porque algún día ellas van a ser una madre para alguien.*"

"What did they say?" she asked the driver.

"We must take extra special care of them, because someday, like you, lady, they're going to be somebody's mommy!"

A Father's Journey

I passed a man walking over the Three-Mile Bridge as I drove from Pensacola, Florida. He had a small suitcase, and I did something I had not done in thirty years. I pulled over and asked him if he wanted a ride across the bridge, even though he was not hitchhiking.

He looked me over, deciding whether he wanted to get into my Jeep. After a moment, he smiled and said, "Yes, that would save me a very windy walk!"

He said he was on his way to see his nine-year-old daughter, Sara Catherine, who lived in Sarasota. He said he hoped to reach her by Christmas Eve. Then he narrated the story of a once-happy marriage, the death of his wife when his daughter was five, his descent into alcoholism, and the loss of his job as a computer programmer. While unemployed, he sent Sara to live with his brother and sister-in-law. They were childless and were raising their niece as their own.

Although he had found work in construction in Hobbs, New Mexico, he hadn't been able to save enough to buy a car. So, he had decided to walk. Taking the byways and avoiding the freeways, it had taken him weeks to get to his destination.

"I've met some very nice people," he said. "I've slept under the stars and, all in all, it's been a mighty pleasant trip."

As I pulled off Highway 98, I took out a hundred-dollar bill and told him, "I'm not giving you this money, because I'm sure you don't need it. But I want you to buy your daughter something nice from Santa Claus."

He looked at me but didn't take it. I smiled and said, "I'll throw it out on the highway if you don't want it. I'm sure someone will find it and buy something nice for a special person."

I rolled down my window, but he took the money before I could toss it. As he got out, he pulled a grade-school photo of Sara from his pocket and gave it to me.

"I'm sure Sara would like Santa to have a picture of her," he said. That grinning photo of Sara sits in a frame on my piano today to remind me about a father's love. Whenever I look at that picture of Sara, I think of a dad who would walk all the way across America just to see his little girl for Christmas.

The Littlest Screw

There was a beautiful and well-kept village. The people were very proud and loyal citizens. One day, they held a meeting to decide what type of monument could be erected on the town square—a final touch—something both useful and lovely. They decided to erect a large hand-carved clock.

They sent for the best materials and employed the finest craftsmen, for they wanted a most impressive landmark that would not tarnish, rust, or warp from the weather.

Finally it was completed, and the entire town came to see the magnificent timepiece. As each walked around the clock looking at the exquisite workmanship, the proud builder explained the hundreds of moving parts—especially the impressive mainspring that made the clock run. When the explanation was finished, the builder joined the mayor on the platform to cut the big red ribbon and make it chime for the first time. The clock began to strike twelve—gong, gong, gong. On the eleventh chime it suddenly stopped. Humiliated and dismayed, the embarrassed builder started to dismantle the clock piece by piece to find the problem.

A minute turned into an hour, yet the supportive townspeople waited for him to fix it. With most of the parts lying in front of him on the platform, the builder finally yelled with glee, "Ah ha, I found the problem!" Expecting to see him hold up a large piece of something, the builder reached deep into the cabinet and pulled out the littlest screw in the clock. He held it up and sheepishly explained, "Wouldn't you know it? The biggest and most obvious things weren't the problem or the solution. The smallest, seemingly insignificant screw has fallen out, which caused the mainspring to malfunction. The entire clockwork depended on the littlest screw. I guess every single ingredient and part in the clock, large and small, is just as important as each of the other parts."

The Hot Tub Theory

I'm sure you've all experienced what I call the "Hot Tub Theory." When you injure an ankle, you're supposed to put it in cold water to immediately stop the swelling. What happens to you when you do this?

First of all, your heart seems to stop. Then you get pains in your leg and neck. Next you lose your breath, get a severe headache, and take your foot out quickly. All of this happens in the space of maybe three seconds and oh, baby, does it hurt! No way will you put your foot back in that ice water! In another instance, you've been injured for a while, and this time the treatment is to get into a hot tub (115 degrees hot!) all the way up to your chin. You think, "Great, this will be relaxing." But no sooner has your body been immersed than you come flying out of the scalding water. It's way too hot for you!

Both cases are interesting and are crucial to the Hot Tub Theory. In fact, they both prove the theory true!

The theory is that you can't bear any extreme temperature all at once. But if you were to get into lukewarm water, get used to it, and then add ice or heat little by little until you reached the desired temperature, you wouldn't feel the shock or notice the temperature change.

Life is the same way. How many times have we been lulled to inertia by a gradual decay in societal values, morals, standards of excellence, and levels of expectation? The lull is found in the three defining elements and consequences of setting expectations. First, when we stretch ourselves and set high expectations, and then work hard to bring our behavior up to meet those high expectation, we call it accomplishment. It makes us feel good and builds our positive self-esteem.

When we become lethargic and apathetic and set low expectations, we bring our motivation and behavior down to meet those low expectations. We call this rationalization. In other words, we make excuses for lack of peak performance.

This is the second element in setting expectations. Rationalization cripples our attempts to meet expectations.

The third element in setting expectations is not setting them at all. It's called procrastination. Have you ever noticed that the longer you put something off, the more difficult it is to get started? This is usually when the lull begins. We think we are comfortable and our attitude is "Chill out. I'm not ready to change right now."

Dive in. Don't wait until things get so backed up that you need a therapist to help you dig your way out. If you attack a project, you'll feel better. And if you keep at it, the long list of things that seemed unbearable will be finished. Take charge of your life and destiny today!

Urgency

I learned about urgency while flying from Dallas, Texas, to Salt Lake City, Utah—approximately a two-hour, fifteen-minute flight. As I boarded and settled into my seat, I noticed the gentleman sitting next to me reading the newspaper account of the United Airlines jetliner that crashed in Iowa in 1989, killing hundreds of passengers. Out of curiosity, I looked over his shoulder and read that the cause of the accident was a failure in the hydraulic system. The pilots lost their ability to steer the aircraft.

I fell asleep at takeoff, only to be awakened about thirty minutes later by the pilot's voice on the PA system. He said, "I'm sure you've noticed that we are lumbering in the sky about seven thousand feet above the ground still on the outskirts of Dallas. We have lost the hydraulic steering system on the aircraft. We will remain airborne for another hour and a half to burn off excess fuel. Then to the best of our ability, we will attempt an emergency landing at the DFW airport. The flight attendants will keep you posted and instruct you in the emergency landing position and procedures when the time comes."

I had a window seat! What a drag! And I was looking down at the ground, thinking, *This could be it.* I always thought that I would die of old age on a golf course! But no, I was going down in a plane crash and only had a couple of hours to live. There was an airphone in the seat in front of me. I entered my credit card number and dialed the first telephone number I thought of.

To take this experience out of the sky and put it on the ground, you need to ask yourself, if you knew that today you were going to be involved in a fatal automobile accident, if you knew that you had two hours to live, would you immediately make a phone call? Who would you call? What would you say? How would you be remembered—as a positive influence who left your family, friends, job, and world in better shape than you found them? Or as a negative pessimist who

205

dragged others down and made your associates miserable and unproductive?

I phoned my mother first. I love my mother. When I was growing up, she always kept me on my toes with wonderful wisdom like, "Don't climb up that tree. If you fall down and break both your legs, don't come running to me!" So I prepared myself. This time she was the concerned financial counselor. "Danny, is that you? You sound a long ways away."

I said, "Yes, Mother dear, I'm on an airplane."

"Isn't that expensive?" she asked.

"Yes, Mom, a few dollars a minute."

"I'm ashamed of you. Who do you think you are, throwing money away like that? This is irresponsible. You hang up right now and phone me when you land."

I said, "No, I need to talk now." I couldn't tell her I was going to crash because she would have probably interrupted with another momism like, "Do you have on clean underwear?"

I did say I had been thinking and feeling many things for quite some time and decided not to procrastinate saying them any longer. I thanked her for going without a new dress so I could have the best football cleats and for postponing family vacations so I could stay home to play on an all-star baseball team—simple things that she thought went unnoticed all these years. I told my mom I loved her and needed her. She started crying, saying, "I love you too." And we hung up.

I then phoned my family and had an intimate conversation, expressing love, need, respect, and support. I have a four-million-dollar life insurance policy, so I definitely wasn't going to tell anyone that I may crash, or they would have already been headed to the mall!

I then phoned my older brother and told him I loved and needed him. He was obviously knocked off guard, thinking I was a bit wiggy. He told me I wasn't in his will, and no, I couldn't have his Bud Light. We laughed at the reference to the old TV commercial, and he confessed, "I love you too, man!" I then phoned my sister, then my younger brother, and a couple of my dearest friends. We all engaged in similar conversations.

The two hours flew by, and we went into DFW Airport on final approach bobbing in the sky with emergency vehicles lining both sides of the runway. After a tense moment, we touched down. No, we didn't crash.

A week later, I got the phone bill. I was so ticked off—at least until I realized the lesson in that two-hour seminar in the sky! I learned about urgency. I learned that today is not the first day of the rest of your life, as they say. It could be the last day of your life, so we had better live it to the fullest. I learned we need to frequently express our love and gratitude for life and everything and everybody in it. We should never leave anything important unsaid. I've been foolish not to have reflected at least once a day on the urgency and real emotions I felt that day on the plane.

Keep Your Fork

A woman had been given three months to live. She contacted her pastor and had him come to her house to discuss certain aspects of her final wishes. She told him which songs she wanted sung at the service, what scriptures she would like read, and what outfit she wanted to be buried in. The woman also requested to be buried with her favorite Bible.

As the pastor was preparing to leave, the woman excitedly proclaimed, "There's one more thing. I want to be buried with a fork in my right hand." The pastor stood looking at the woman, not knowing quite what to say.

"That surprises you, doesn't it?" the woman asked.

"Well, to be honest, I'm puzzled by the request," said the pastor.

The woman explained, "In all my years of attending church socials and potluck dinners, I always remember that when the dishes of the main course were being cleared, someone would inevitably lean over and say, 'Keep your fork.' It was my favorite part because I knew that something better was coming, like velvety chocolate cake or deep-dish apple pie. Something wonderful and with substance! So, I just want people to see me there in that casket with a fork in my hand and wonder. Then I want you to tell them, 'Keep your fork. The best is yet to come.'"

The pastor's eyes welled up with tears of joy as he hugged the woman goodbye. He knew this would be one of the last times he would see her before her death. But he also knew that the woman had a better grasp of heaven than he did. She knew that something better was coming.

At the funeral, people were walking by the woman's casket, and sure enough, over and over, the pastor heard the question "What's with the fork?" And over and over he smiled. During his message, he told them about the fork and what it symbolized to her.

"In conclusion," the pastor said. "I trust the next time you are at a meal and reach down for your fork, it will remind you, oh so gently, that no matter what your past has been, you have a spotless future. The best is yet to come!"

Commitment

What Do You See?

Inspiration is nothing more than "possibility thinking." To inspire is to have dreams for sale, to keep hope alive, to outwardly express faith to help others see what they cannot see, and to openly suggest that the best is yet to be. A nurse shared the following true story with me.

John and Bill became acquainted during their care at the Huntsman Cancer Institute in Salt Lake City. Separated by only a curtain, they both shared the same treatment room one day during a unique chemotherapy treatment. John had been in the hospital for a while and was so sick that he was stuck flat on his back. As a result of several surgeries and because of the way he was hooked up to machines, John was taken to a private room where he would most likely stay for the next month.

The two men never saw each other, but they became instant friends as they talked and even laughed through their painful ordeal. As the three hours of intravenous treatment ended, they said their good-byes, but not before Bill promised to drop by John's room in the morning to visit.

Sure enough, the following day, an orderly picked Bill up and wheeled him from his room to John's room. John was flat on his back and could not see Bill come in. Bill was not allowed to get close to John's bed, so he entered and immediately took up a position by the window. "Hey, John," Bill greeted. "How ya feeling? Man, it's a beautiful day. I'm sitting here at your window in my wheelchair, and my oh my, it is gorgeous."

John replied, "Hey, buddy. Thanks for coming. Tell me what you see, my friend."

"Oh my gosh, John, the flowers are red and white and look like a flag. The grass is lime green with perfectly cut, eighteen-inch-high hedges serving as an elegant border to the sidewalk for as far as I can see. There are two hummingbirds hovering by the windowsill and a big white cat lurking on the fence. Someday when we can open the window, or better still, get out of here, you will again hear the cheerful chirping of the three robins in the tree, and I will take you fishing on a breathtaking, blue, cloudless sky day just like today!"

For thirty minutes, John got excited and then thanked Bill for sharing the outside world with him. "Being confined in here really gets depressing, and though I can't go to the world, you have brought the world to me. Thank you, thank you, my new friend."

As Bill was wheeled out of the room, again not being allowed to get close enough for eye contact, the two men exchanged their love and support.

"Will I see you tomorrow?" John pleaded.

"You can count on it, old buddy."

The next day, Bill was wheeled in again by the orderly and parked by the window in John's room. They exchanged pleasantries and Bill spoke up. "Holy cow, John. You should see the fancy cars parked in the parking lot. These doctors are driving some fine rides. No wonder they wear surgical masks. They charge so much they don't want us to see who they really are!"

They laughed and laughed! Bill continued. "There's a stereotypical red Ferrari. Oh, and look over there at that black Porsche and lavender Corvette. I guess if you've got a Corvette, you think you are so much of a stud that you can actually drive a 'foo-foo' colored car!" They both laughed again.

"Wow, with the mist from the lawn sprinklers, I can actually see a rainbow," Bill continued. "Just like us, buddy. You've got to have a storm in order to have a rainbow. When we weather this cancer storm and get out of here, with all your money you can buy me a Lamborghini, and we'll go pick up some babes! Money matters when you're bald and ugly like me."

They both laughed again, and after the usual thirty-minute visit, Bill was wheeled back to his room without John seeing him. This visiting went on for seven days straight. Unbeknownst to John, Bill was taken in for surgery on the eighth day. John waited all day and into the night, but Bill did not come. The next morning an oncologist and a nurse who had never treated John before came to administer tests. John spoke up, "Doc, do you happen to know my friend Bill Johnson?" The doctor and the nurse both cringed and said, "Friend? How do you know Mr. Johnson?" John explained how they had met and how, for the past week, Bill had been wheeled into his room every morning and had sat by the window, describing in detail what he saw as he lovingly opened up the outside world to John.

The nurse gently took John by the hand and said, "I'm sorry, John. Yesterday, Bill had his long-awaited operation, and the surgery didn't go as well as we had hoped. We did all we could do. Bill passed away in the evening with his family around him. We didn't know you were such good friends, or someone would have told you."

John started to cry. "I've been confined on my back in this prisonlike predicament for so long I had lost all hope and desire to fight my cancer and get better. Then Bill came along. Every day he came to my room and helped me see what I could not. He painted beautiful word pictures full of colors, sounds, and dreams. He allowed me to see a brighter day through his eyes. Oh, how I will miss him sitting at my window describing a world that made me look forward to getting better."

The nurse and the doctor again looked at each other as the nurse quietly spoke. "Isn't that interesting, John. Your friend Bill was totally blind."

Friendship

There once was a little boy who had a bad temper. His teacher gave him a bag of nails and told him that every time he lost his temper at school, he must hammer a nail into the old fence on the vacant lot behind the school. By the end of the first day, the boy had driven thirty-seven nails into the fence. Over the next few weeks, as he learned to control his anger, the number of nails hammered daily dwindled. He discovered that it was easier to hold his temper than to drive those nails into the fence.

Finally, the day came when the boy didn't lose his temper at all. He told his teacher about it, and the teacher suggested that the boy now pull out one nail for each day that he was able to hold his temper. The days passed, and the young boy was finally able to tell his teacher that all the nails were gone.

The teacher took the lad by the hand and led him to the fence. She said, "You have done well, my son, but look at the holes in the fence. The fence will never be the same. When you say things in anger, they leave a scar just like this one. You can put a knife in a man and draw it out. It doesn't matter how many times you say you're sorry; the wound is still there. A verbal wound is as bad as a physical one. Friends are very rare. Most of us are lucky to have one or two good friends in an entire lifetime. They make us smile and encourage us to succeed. They lend an ear, they share words of praise, and they always want to open their hearts to us."

To have a friend, you must first be a friend. A best friend brings out the best in you and you in them. Let us show our friends how much we care!

The Wrong Foot

Some people seem to start life out on the wrong foot. Let me tell you about one girl who was lucky to even get out of the starting block at all.

She was born prematurely at four pounds. By the age of four, doctors discovered a double attack of pneumonia, and scarlet fever had crippled her left leg. At age eight, she finally began to regain the use of her leg. After two years of therapy three times a week, she was finally able to limp. With a special brace, she could walk by age twelve.

But she didn't want to just walk. She wanted to run, and run faster than any woman ever before her. By the time she was fifteen, she was running well enough to become the star of her high school's track and basketball teams. She won a track scholarship to Tennessee State University.

In 1960, she made the U.S. Olympic team and won three gold medals in Rome. She won the 100-meter and the 200-meter dashes in world record time. Then she anchored the 4 × 100-meter relay team for a world record win. All this from a sickly girl who was never supposed to run at all!

Wilma Rudolph was named America's Female Athlete of the Year. The woman who got out of the starting blocks faster than any woman ever had almost didn't get out of the blocks at all.

But there's more than a history lesson to this story. Remember, it doesn't matter where you begin, only where you end up. The people who believe that and act according to what they believe live dreams they could only imagine. Every successful champion in every field of endeavor started somewhere. And even if they started on the wrong foot, they finished a winner.

Musical Influence

Music changes our behavior. If you are driving down the highway and Barry Manilow comes on the radio, what are you going to do? Change the station, throw up, rip the radio out of the car?

Some people listen to this music, and you can always tell who they are. They are driving down the highway going twenty-five miles an hour. Their left-hand blinker has been on for fifty miles (no one dares to pass them because this turn might be it!). They have shut their car door on their overcoat and the belt is hanging out the door, dangling and bouncing off the pavement. They are singing along with absolutely no clue about what is going on outside their car. "Mandy, oh Mandy," they sing.

I had a crazy friend in high school who used to go to Kentucky Fried Chicken and collect those little tubs of coleslaw that no one ever eats. When he thought it was appropriate, he threw them at things. I can just see this couple driving slowly along singing "Mandy, Mandy" and Brian throwing the coleslaw. Splat! Squish all over the windshield. The driver turns to his wife, "Oh my gosh, Ethel, what kind of a bug was that?"

Now think about how music changes your behavior. You are driving down the road listening to mellow music and going twenty-five miles an hour. Suddenly, Guns and Roses comes on the radio. Without even thinking about it, you are now driving ninety-five miles an hour in a school zone! Little children are diving into the bushes, and you are headbanging all the way home!

Work for the Company

It's been prophetically written: "Without vision, people perish." This observation is blatantly obvious in the National Football League.

Certain teams are perennial champions, and others are perennial losers. Why? The answer came when the players on the last- and first-place teams were interviewed and asked, "Why are you here?" The last-place players' eyes were downcast. They mumbled excuses for their poor playing as if their cholesterol count was higher than their SAT scores. They each answered the question by saying, "I'm here to play football." Observe the operative word *I'm*.

Contrast these losers with the champions. When the powerhouse players were questioned, they stood taller, with confidence and enthusiasm oozing from every pore. They knew their purpose and they expected positive results. When asked, "Why are you here?" they boldly proclaimed, "We're here to win the Super Bowl!"

Can you see the difference?

The losers had no vision. They were content to be in a mediocre, short-term survival mode just hanging on to finish the season and pay the bills. The winners had vision. They focused on purpose instead of just setting goals. They want it all and are willing to work hard toward achieving that long-term peak-performance result.

What is your vision—both personally and careerwise? Where will you be in five, ten, or twenty years? Are you working for a paycheck or working for the company? Do you only look forward to Friday instead of to every day of the week? Do you think you are paid by the hour, or do you realize that you are paid for the value you bring to that hour?

Young people give up opportunities to get good grades and participate in extracurricular activities at school just to work for minimum wage so they can have a fancy car or nice clothes. The sad truth, is they will struggle the rest of their lives. An education allows them to have options so they can get the job of their dreams instead of settling for the leftovers. All of us need a long-term vision! What is yours?

Legacy

Tribute to Preparation

Wayne Gretzky is clearly the greatest hockey player to ever play the game. He has influenced the lives of many young players. Wayne says that the greatest single influence in his life is his father, Walter. Walt was his coach, his mentor, and has always been and will always be his best friend. Wayne's greatest honor comes when he is introduced as Walter Gretzky's son.

I had the honor of talking with Wayne, but the greatest thrill was spending two days with Walter in his home in Brantford, Ontario, Canada. We played golf; laughed; toured his famous basement full of Wayne's MVP awards, trophies, autographed sticks, skates, and jerseys; laughed some more; and swapped countless inspirational stories. Walt is extremely smart and very intense, yet warm and engaging. He is a deeply committed family man and is community-oriented in his tireless efforts to help charitable organizations. Even today, he coaches junior hockey teams and touches hundreds of young people's lives each year. With Walt as his dad, it is obvious why Wayne is such a clean, powerful, positive role model and an elegant gentleman.

Walt is famous for saying, "You miss 100 percent of the shots you don't take." Wayne is famous for answering the question, "Why are you the greatest player?" with the highly quoted response, "Most players go to where the puck is. I go to where the puck is going to be." Yes, Wayne Gretzky teaches us about anticipation, but, according to his dad, Wayne teaches us even more about preparation.

If you want to discover why Wayne is the greatest hockey player who ever lived, don't watch him on the ice—watch him when he is on the bench. He studies every player to see where they go, how they pass, to whom they pass, which side they favor, how they fight, if they can defend going backward, and who they favor in certain playmaking situations. By the time Wayne hits the ice, he knows exactly where to go to intercept a pass, where to block a shot, and when to skate into the spacing lanes of the other team to get the competitive advantage to shoot and score. Preparation is why Wayne Gretzky is hockey's all-time leading scorer.

Walt told me Wayne was also an exceptional baseball player. Wayne was named to the all-star team every year since he was nine years old. He was an extraordinary pitcher. Wayne wanted to practice every day, but most of his friends were out doing the playful things little guys like to do—riding bikes, hiking, catching lizards. So Wayne would bribe his friends by paying them a quarter to play goalie while he took 100 shots and another quarter to catch while he threw 100 pitches. These kids would oftentimes go home with sore hands, black eyes, and bloody noses from their inability to stop his extremely hard, fast shots and pitches. By the time Wayne was a teenager, he had a ninety-mile-an-hour fastball. Walt told me it was amazing to watch Wayne pitch. Even if the batters hit against him in the first couple of innings, by the time Wayne had faced each of them once, he remembered their strengths and weaknesses and struck them out from then on.

Walt told me Wayne is a perfectionist and used to practice the same shot from the same place on the ice hundreds of times in an afternoon. When most kids lost interest and concentration, Wayne would somehow kick it into a higher gear and endure until he succeeded at what he was trying to accomplish. He even practiced hitting the puck off certain places in the hockey rink baseboards so he would know exactly where the puck was going to be when it ricocheted. Wayne's desire to prepare was so intense that he convinced his dad to build a hockey rink in the backyard and flood it in the winter, which allowed Wayne to start practicing at the crack of dawn and continue until the neighbors complained late at night about the noise. The only thing that took Wayne off the ice was his dad's reminder that he needed to go to bed and rest so he could wake up refreshed, alert, and ready to do it again the next day.

Having met Wayne, I can say that his preparation philosophy of "leaving no regrets" paid its greatest dividend when his dear, sweet dad had a brain aneurysm at the age of fifty-four. When Wayne received the late-night emergency phone call in Los Angeles, he rushed to be at his dying father's bedside. When he arrived, the doctors told Wayne there was very little hope.

Wayne ignored the prognosis and sat for hours and hours talking to his dad and stroking his arm. He found strength in the knowledge that he had no regrets. He had said all the things he needed to say to his hero many times before this tragedy occurred. He had already spent more time with his dad than most children spend with their dads in an entire lifetime. Clearly, Wayne was prepared for the worst, which allowed him to be strong for others and focus his energy on praying, hoping, and coaxing his dad to hang tough and pull through. Even more important than Wayne's preparation, however, was the fact that the nurses were prepared, and the hospital staff was prepared, and a specialist doctor—who was one of the only physicians in the world prepared to perform the intricate surgery—was willing to come out of retirement because he was prepared.

Walter Gretzky miraculously recovered and remains the number one influence in Wayne's life today. And the message? Preparation not only gave Wayne his life, it also saved Walter from death. Gretzky is not the greatest hockey player who ever lived simply because he can anticipate. Wayne is the Great One because his dad taught him to relentlessly pursue perfection through preparation.

I Am the Greatest

Cassius Marcellus Clay Jr., as Muhammad Ali was once known, was born in Louisville, Kentucky, on January 17, 1942. During Ali's youth, Louisville was a city of segregated public facilities, the Kentucky Derby, and other symbols of the Southern white aristocracy. African Americans were the servants and poor working class. The grandest dreams available to them were being a preacher or a teacher in an all-black church or school.

Young Cassius was intense and full of dreams, which in this environment brought frustration. He knew he was somebody and needed to somehow vent his societal suppression. That's when he discovered boxing. At twelve years of age and eighty-nine pounds, young Cassius had his first official boxing match. He won by a split decision and immediately started jumping up and down yelling, "I am the greatest. I will be the greatest fighter who ever lived."

Years later, a childhood classmate remembered, "We were in elementary school together and Cassius was just another one of the kids. You push and you shove each other, and get into the normal fights. There were days he lost and days he won. So when he beat Sonny Liston to win the heavyweight championship, we all started laughing, saying, 'He's not even undefeated in the neighborhood. How can he be champion of the world?'"

I can't exactly explain why, but probably the most prestigious award, accomplishment, or title in all of sports is to win the heavyweight boxing championship of the world. Cassius Clay won the championship, converted to the Muslim faith, changed his name to Muhammad Ali, was stripped of his title for refusing induction into the US Army on religious grounds, and won the championship back two more times. He truly is the greatest. He is not only the most famous fighter who ever lived, but the most famous athlete and most recognized face in the world.

As a teenager, I had been a Golden Gloves boxer, and Ali had been my idol. I emulated everything he did from tassels on my boots to the Ali Shuffle, rope-a-dope, and taunting jab. With fast hands and a desire to beat everybody, I was known as the "Great White Hope." Each time I fought, instead of chanting, "Danny, Danny," my friends chanted, "Dali, Dali!" Muhammad Ali truly was my hero, and I would have given anything to meet him.

Years later, in 1988, I had just finished speaking to the students of Andrews University in Berrien Springs, Michigan. I was in the Union Building signing books when I overheard some students talking about seeing Muhammad Ali on campus. I was so excited I could hardly ask where. They informed me that he was gone, but it was no big deal because he lived there and visited the school often. I immediately excused myself and asked the two gentlemen who were driving me around to grab a camera and take me to Ali's home. They told me I was fooling myself if I thought I could meet him. They stopped at the big white wall and giant iron gate at the edge of a long, curving driveway. I got out and walked the hundred yards to his beautiful home. His eighty-eight acres had previously belonged to the Chicago gangster Al Capone, and "Muhammad Ali Farms," as Ali called it, was an amazing sight.

With my heart pounding, I took a deep breath and knocked on the front door. A beautiful woman answered. I knew from photographs that she was his lovely wife. She asked, "May I help you?" I said, "Yes ma'am. Is Muhammad in?" She asked, "May I tell him who is calling?" Sheepishly, I replied, "Sure, Dan Clark." She walked away, and within seconds, an imposing six-foot-three-inch, 225-pound world champion, world peace ambassador, advocate of human rights, living legend, and idol filled the entire doorway. Muhammad simply smiled his famous smile and in his quiet, breathy voice invited me in. I excused myself for a minute, sprinted to the garden to where my friends could see me and wildly waved my arms and whistled for them to come in.

In 1988, Muhammad's Parkinson's disease had not yet taken away his speech. Although he was a little slow, he talked up a storm. The next four and a half hours, we sat in his living room and watched his greatest fights: the Thrilla in Manila, the Rumble in the Jungle, and more. With his own personal commentary, jokes, and stories, he made every move come alive. Later he even performed some of his favorite magic tricks.

The most incredible thing for me was when he asked me, "Did you ever fight?" I nodded yes, and he said, "Let me see your left hook." We both put our hands up and started to playfully spar and dance around. I broke into the Ali Shuffle, and he kidded me, "That's not the Shuffle, that's the Clark Scuffle!" He then got right in my face and said, "Everybody knows I'm the greatest, but so are you. Repeat with me, 'I am the greatest.'" I repeated it and he said, "Louder, with more heart." I repeated it, and he said, "No, like your man Rocky. Mean it, man, mean it. Say it like you want to beat Joe Frazier. Say it like you want to punch George Foreman. Say it to me like I'm Howard Cosell!" One more time he yelled, "I am the greatest," and again had me mimic him. He then put his arm around me, gave me a big hug, looked me square in the eyes, and whispered, "How do you feel? Do you believe it? I do."

It's been many years since that wonderful day, but I remember it every time I walk past the photos of us hung on my basement "Wall of Fame." Whenever I am discouraged and feel that I can't go on anymore, I relive Ali looking me square in the eyes and convincing me that, "I am the greatest." I guarantee he is, and he wants each of us to believe that we can be, too.

True Nobility

A king sent word into the village that he was in search of a new court counselor and confidant. The first subject was escorted in and the king inquired what he had done. The man knelt and rattled off his résumé as an architect and mathematician who had designed the castle and the bridge with complicated statistics, plans, and logic. He claimed he could counsel the king on how and why we do what we do.

The second subject was announced and the king inquired of his qualifications. The man knelt and explained that he was the one who had built the castle and the bridge. He could counsel the king and his people on the necessity of having a firm foundation and strong pillars to support them in everything they do.

The third subject was brought in, and the king asked what he had done to qualify for the king's court. He knelt and bragged about his legal and medical degrees. He said he could obviously counsel the king on what was broken and how to fix it.

Distraught and disgusted with the egos and self-centered attitudes of each of them, the king reluctantly invited in the final subject. When he saw an old white-haired woman enter the room, he lost his patience and sarcastically inquired what she could have possibly done. Quietly she answered, "I was their teacher." In response to this, the king rose, stepped down from his throne, and humbly knelt at her feet to pay tribute to the noblest profession of all. Teaching is the profession that makes all other professions possible!

Take It Personally

The greatest educator, Horace Mann, was asked to be the guest speaker at a dedication service for a beautiful new high school building. Standing on the stage of a state-of-the-art auditorium, he concluded by gesturing and saying, "All the sacrifice, hard work, time, and money that went into this magnificent edifice will be worth it if we but help one child."

As Mr. Mann was exiting the building, a parent confronted him. "Didn't you overstate it a little, that all this would be worth it if we just help one child?" the parent asked. Horace Mann, in his wisdom, simply replied, "No. What if that child was yours?!"

The next time we complain against tax levies and bond issues to improve our school systems, let us take it personally and vote *yes* for education!

Born to Succeed

Think about the concept, "You were born to succeed." Do you believe it?

Recently, I went down to a local hospital to visit my friends and see their new baby. Peeking through the window of the nursery, I couldn't help but think that each child was born to succeed. They all goo-gooed and ga-gaed basically the same, no accents, no political preferences, different races, different sexes, unique, one-of-a-kind bodies and faces, but all born to succeed.

As I left that beautiful environment full of innocent, precious children, I got into my car to go home and ended up driving by the post office downtown. When I stopped at the intersection to wait for the red light to turn green, I glanced over, and there, leaning up against the wall of a building, were what I guessed to be three homeless men under the influence, totally oblivious to the world around them. As usual, I thought to myself, *Whoa, that's sad.* I wondered what happened to them and what could have been done differently. Just before the light changed, I turned my head to the other side of the road and saw two immaculately dressed, successful-looking women flanking a successful-looking man, walking arm-in-arm out of a building entrance. "Attorneys at Law" was printed across the top of the door.

All of a sudden, it hit me like a ton of bricks. The three experiences magically meshed together to fully explain this principle: "We were born to succeed." The pure, benevolent babies in the hospital nursery, the three down-and-out men, and the three polished professionals all had one thing in common. Simply, they are human beings. Never once has a mother brought into the world anything other than a boy or a girl. Never once has a mother brought into the world a high school dropout or a college graduate, a drug user, gang member, doctor, teacher, lawyer, or world-class athlete. Who we are and what we become after we leave the hospital nursery is a direct result of who we think we can become.

Handle with Care

Scott took a long look at his speedometer before slowing down: 53 in a 20 mile-an-hour zone ... fourth time in as many months. How could a guy get caught so often, this time in a school zone? Scott pulled over and immediately began to plan his excuse. As the cop stepped out of his car, Scott noticed it was Jim from church. Scott sunk into his sport coat as he had never seen Jim in his uniform. This was worse than the coming ticket. A Christian cop catching a guy from his own church who happened to be a little eager to get home after a long day at the office. A guy he was about to play golf with tomorrow at the church opening social.

Jim was also surprised to see Scott, a man he saw every Sabbath. "Fancy meeting you like this," Scott sheepishly said.

"Hello, Scott." No smile.

"Guess you caught me red-handed in a rush to see my wife and kids," Scott commented.

"Yes, I guess," Jim seemed uncertain.

Scott continued to try to talk his way out of the ticket. "I've seen some long days at the office lately. I'm afraid I bent the rules a bit—just this once." Jim wouldn't give eye contact and kicked at the gravel on the shoulder of the road.

Scott continued to mount his defense, "Ann said something about Irish stew and chocolate cheesecake tonight. I was in a hurry but I wasn't going that fast. What did you clock me at, 30 in the 20?" The lie seemed to come easier with every ticket. Jim was undaunted and scribbled away on his ticket pad.

Scott was flustered. Why hadn't Jim asked for a driver's license? Whatever the reason, it would be a month of Sundays before Scott ever sat near this cop again. A tap on the door jerked Scott's head to the left. There was Jim with a folded paper in hand. Scott rolled down the window a mere two inches, just enough room for Jim to pass him the slip.

"Thanks," Scott sarcastically responded as Jim returned to his car without a word. Fuming in anger, Scott waited until Jim drove away before he opened the slip. How much was this one going to cost?

Scott was startled. Was this some kind of a joke? Certainly not a ticket. He began to read.

Dear Scott:

I had a son. An only son. He was eight when killed by a car. You guessed it—a speeding driver through a school zone. A fine and three months in jail, and the man was free. Free to hug his own sons. All four of them. I only had one, and I'm going to have to wait until heaven before I can ever hug him again. Seventy times seven I've tried to forgive that man. A thousand times I thought I had. Maybe I did, but I need to do it again. Even now. Pray for me to be compassionate, and be careful. I miss my little guy so much and would give anything to have him back.

Jim

Scott sat there in shock—crying. Alone. Growing with new resolve. A full fifteen minutes later, he too pulled away and drove slowly home, praying for forgiveness and hugging a surprised wife and kids when he arrived. Life is sacred, precious, fragile—handle with care.

Dream

A man had a dream one night that an angel appeared to him. The angel told the man that because he had lived a noble life, he would grant him one wish. After contemplating the possibilities, the man decided to ask for love, peace, and happiness to fill the whole earth. In response to his wish, the angel answered, "That's good, sir, but we don't deal in fruits here, we only deal in seeds." The dream ended.

This is true in real life. When you think about it, our society concentrates more on fruit problems than on seed solutions to the problems. If we are ever going to change and make a better world for ourselves, we need to dig through the fruits of failures and find the seeds of success.

Alcohol, drunk driving, drug abuse, violence, lack of respect for authority, and suicide are not the problems; they are only the fruits. They come as a result of actions caused by bad seeds. It's all about the law of the harvest—we reap what we sow. If we plant corn, we cannot harvest wheat. If we play a tuned piano and press the C key, an F sound will not come out. Input equals output 100 percent of the time. We reap what we sow.

All of our emphasis, time, and talents seem to be spent on the rehabilitation of bad fruits instead of working with preventative measures at the seed level. Doesn't it seem much wiser to build a fence at the edge of the cliff than to park an ambulance at its base? Wouldn't it be better if we worked hard to get it right the first time?

As each of us weaves our way through life, we are faced with fulfilling three basic needs: the need to feel love, the need to feel wanted and important, and the need to feel a true sense of security. As humans, we will do almost anything to satisfy these three basic needs. We'll change our hairstyles and dress codes, alter our moral standards, compromise our health habits and beliefs, and change nearly anything in order to fulfill these needs. It's sad, but look around and see that it's true! Different hairstyles, unique clothing, alcohol, drunk driving, drug abuse, violence, and lack of respect for authority are the residual effects of a person trying to fulfill his or her needs. We are all crying from within, "praise me, punish me, yell at me, ground me, kick me out of class, arrest me, but don't you dare ignore me. Please notice me. I'm important too. And if I can't get attention for doing something good, powerful, positive, and productive, I will do something negative to satisfy my needs."

The next time you do or say something negative, or the next time you hear or see someone else say or do something negative, remember the negative action was created by a deeper negative cause. Fix the cause. Replant the seed and you change the harvested fruit.

Military

To Thine Own Self Be True

Everyone was in awe of Seth Goldberg's principles, values, inner strength, and total peace of mind. As a devout Jew, he was faithful to his beliefs and true to himself. Even though he was mellow, Goldberg was definitely not a passive soldier. When it came to fighting the enemy, he was always the first to volunteer for the terrifying missions. In fact, Goldberg saved the life of every man in his platoon at least once. He was a highly decorated soldier at the end of World War II, and his story will help each of us put the war in its proper perspective.

Because Goldberg was a true hero in every sense of the word, you would think that he would have received many promotions and become a high-ranking officer during the war. Quite the contrary. The officers were afraid to promote Goldberg because he had the reputation of being a German-lover. Even though he was Jewish, he didn't hate the Germans like everyone else. He said they were about the same as us, perhaps a little bit more hardheaded, but basically the same. He said they had wives and girlfriends and families who loved them and prayed for their well-being just as we had. Goldberg was not only empathetic, but he also spoke excellent German. Just before the war broke out, Goldberg had attended college for three years in Germany, where his German roommate became his best friend.

If Goldberg liked the Germans so much, how was he able to fight them so well? He simply replied, "The only way to stop the evil, corrupt Hitler and his Nazis is to defeat the German people who have let themselves be deceived by Hitler." He said it was wrong to kill the Germans, but it was more wrong for Hitler and his Nazis to annihilate innocent people and deceive the entire world. Goldberg said that sometimes, we are forced to choose between two evils, and Hitler had to be stopped at all costs.

Once, Goldberg stayed up all night trying to save the life of a young German soldier who had a bullet in his chest. The boy died the next morning, and his fellow soldiers saw a tear in Goldberg's eye as he began digging the grave.

Seth Goldberg's final story unfolded a few months after that incident took place. In it lies the true nature of war.

The platoon next to his caught a German trying to steal supplies. One of their men was injured while arresting the German. The captors brought the German to their camp on the way to the brig, and as the light of the fire illuminated his face, Goldberg sprang to his feet. The muscles in his neck and arms were bulging and tense. He shook his head and blinked his eyes to confirm what he saw. Then he leaped toward the German. The guard's first reaction should have been to protect the German, for it wasn't uncommon for a soldier to try to kill a prisoner when he remembered that the prisoner had killed one of his buddies. But in this instance, that was not the case. Before anyone had a chance to do anything, Goldberg and the prisoner were hugging and kissing each other on the cheek as they exchanged a few words in German. Everyone watched in stunned amazement. That is, everyone except the guard, who shouted, *"Weiterlaufen sch wein."* The German broke Goldberg's grip and resumed walking toward the brig. The guard looked at Goldberg and said, "You ought to be shot, you pig-lover."

The only thing that kept Goldberg from smashing the guard in the mouth was his deeply instilled respect for authority. He turned around. Every muscle in his body quivered, and he clenched his fists so tightly that his palms began to bleed. He sat back down and just stared at the ground.

The captain received word of the episode and immediately ordered Goldberg to report to his tent. Tents are not soundproof, and everyone within the immediate vicinity clearly heard the captain order Goldberg to be the fifth man on the sunrise firing squad.

When Goldberg came out of the tent, the men asked him what he was going to do. They reminded him that his refusal to obey a direct order would result in his being shot himself. Goldberg replied, "I understand the consequences, but how can I shoot my best friend, the man who was my college roommate? How can I shoot a man my family loves—a man who has a wife and kids, a man who actually has changed my life for the better?"

So what did Seth Goldberg do? Before I tell you the rest of the story, what do you think you would have done? It would be hard to shoot your best friend, but the German was going to die regardless of whether you personally pulled the trigger. Refusing to shoot would mean that two men would die instead of one. What good would you be to your country if you were dead? On the other hand, what kind of life would you have if you knew that you knowingly had served on the firing squad that executed your best friend?

If you understand the rules of war, you will argue that Goldberg's role in the firing squad wouldn't make him guilty of the German's death. The German would die as a victim of martial law, and Goldberg, as a participant in martial law, would be acting as a soldier and not a murderer.

The end of the story? Early the next morning, the firing squad executed both Seth Goldberg and the German soldier who had been his best friend.

Let us all seriously contemplate Seth Goldberg's legacy—the blatant reminder of the brutal ramifications of war—so that we no longer think of it in terms of country against country or one political system and its leaders against another. War is common person against common person—man, woman, and family against man, woman, and family. We, as brothers and sisters in the family of man, need to love, tolerate, and mutually respect one another. Only then can we "give peace a chance."

In honor of Seth Goldberg, let each of us identify what principle we would be willing to die for and then passionately live for that principle every day. Only then can each of us claim, as did Seth Goldberg, "To mine own self I have been true."

One of the Few Good Men

My experience one Saturday afternoon at the Iwo Jima Memorial Monument made it perfectly clear that our Revolutionary War for life, liberty, and the pursuit of happiness changed the trade, commerce, opportunities, standard of living, and history not just of the Western Hemisphere, but also of the whole world. When the taxi pulled up to the memorial, I got out and told the driver to wait. I only wanted to read the plaque, take a photo, and return to my hotel.

As I walked around the circular drive, I noticed that all of the other tourists were gathered to one side, standing off in a state of shock and awe. I looked over and there, sitting in a wheelchair, was a young, clean-cut man proudly wearing a gold United States Marine Corps t-shirt. His right arm had been blown off and was freshly bandaged. His left arm was also blown off, and one leg—stitched, stapled, and skin-grafted together—was also bandaged.

A solider and his wife were attending to him and were quickly preparing to take his photograph. When they said, "Okay," the young marine struggled to stand on his feet, determined and quaking with more pride than I had seen in a long while. He stood tall and straight, flexed his neck, and bowed his back for the picture. With tears streaming down our cheeks, all of us tourists (about twenty) started to reverently clap and give this courageous young man a standing ovation.

Losing strength, the young marine collapsed into his wheelchair, and his friends pushed him to their car to take him back to the hospital. The young marine looked over at us, saluted, said thank you, and turned to go.

He said "Thank you"? No, Thank you!, I thought. I couldn't refrain myself. Humbly, I caught up to him and with all the love and respect I could muster, I introduced myself, explained that I was emotionally moved and inspired by what I had just experienced, told him that he was a hero, and thanked him for his sacrifice and service. He asked me what I did for a living. When I told him, he said he had read one of my books. That opened the door for me to ask him if he would share his story.

"My name is Corporal James Wright—my friends call me Eddie—United States Marine Corps, one of the few and the proud," he said.

Eddie was twenty-eight years old with a serious girlfriend and was in his second tour of duty in Iraq when he was wounded. A tour lasts six months, with an additional month to overlap with new units arriving.

He told me that he was the only marine at Walter Reed Hospital. His friend Robert Storm, also a marine who had already done two tours in Iraq and was soon returning for another seven months, had flown out from Camp Pendleton in San Diego to visit him. Eddie's accident happened in April. It was now May, and he was excited to be out of the hospital and in the fresh air for the first time since he left Iraq.

Eddie was in a reconnaissance battalion that went out on patrol at least once every day. Their job was to constantly show a presence of strength and security in the toughest parts in and around Baghdad. When reports of insurgents came in, his unit would be sent to the firefight.

A patrol was usually six vehicles—all armored-up Humvees—called a platoon, with four marines inside each vehicle and a machine gunner on top. This particular day, they were on the west side of the city when they came down a road and realized all hell was about to break loose. The soldiers say you know an ambush is coming because suddenly the busy street goes vacant and people hurry off like rats scampering on a sinking ship.

The insurgents greatly outnumbered the marines and opened fire in what is called an "L" ambush, where they shoot from two sides. Eddie was sitting in the passenger rear seat and stuck his SAW (squad automatic weapon) outside and returned fire. Suddenly, a rocket-propelled grenade hit his door. The huge explosion blew Corporal Eddie's right hand off and his left arm off at the elbow. His right leg was ripped apart, destroying thigh muscle and the ability to move his right foot.

His company commander was killed, and though Eddie was gushing blood and dying by the minute, as second in command, he had the responsibility of taking charge and leading the platoon out of the firefight. Marines are taught to fight through attacks, and because it was an "L" ambush, Eddie's platoon had to continue toward the insurgents before they could turn around and fight their way back out. Under Eddie's courageous and unbelievable leadership, they not only killed every one of the attacking insurgents, but they were also able to get back to base with only one dead and a few wounded.

Visualize this if you can: Eddie's arms and part of his leg are blown off, and he still rises to the occasion because others are counting on him. While losing strength, he still yells out orders and directions to his teammates to fight the hard fight, win the battle, and return with honor. For outstanding bravery, going beyond the call of duty, and absolute heroism, Corporal James "Eddie" Wright—United States Marine Corps, one of the few and the proud—was awarded the Bronze Star, the fourth-highest award given in the armed services and presented by President George W. Bush.

It was a sunny Saturday afternoon, but this one day made me more proud, more patriotic, and more dedicated to giving more of myself to duty, honor, country, community, schools, charity, family, and friends. I asked Eddie if he was bitter. He struggled, shook, and again stood up out of his wheelchair on his one good but weak leg, looked me square in the eye, and said, "No sir, I'm not angry. But unless we stay there and finish what we went there to do, I sacrificed my body and left my arms in Baghdad for nothing! I chose to be an American soldier. All of us currently serving in the military are volunteers who enlisted during war. We all knew what we were getting ourselves into. None of us is complaining. I wish parents like that blond lady who is organizing anti-Bush and antiwar demonstrations who lost her marine son would shut her mouth. She's embarrassing her dead son, who is proud he served and willingly sacrificed his life for freedom!

"It's a great feeling to believe in and be part of something that is larger than yourself! I am proud to be a marine and honored to serve my country. If they would let me go back to Iraq, I would go in a minute to be back with my unit. I love and miss those brave men."

Afterward, we had our picture taken together. That photo is the most important photo hanging on my "Wall of Fame."

Eddie's girlfriend, Donnette, stuck by his side; they are now engaged to be married. Today he has prosthetic arms. His right leg is healing, although he will walk with a limp for the rest of his life. Eddie told me twice how lucky he was just to be alive and how thankful he was to have played a small part in bringing freedom, the right to vote, opportunity, and justice to the wonderful Iraqi people.

When I asked him what message I could deliver to the world on his behalf, Eddie looked me in the eye, choked up, gritted his teeth, and said, "Tell them to stay strong and no matter what, not to quit. Tell CNN to report only the truth. The media should not make it look like and sound like the terrorists are winning, because they aren't. Tell the celebrities to shut up—they don't know what they are taking about. Remind U.S. citizens that Islamic fundamentalists have vowed to kill all infidels and Americans, and that it's better to fight them over there than in New York City, Washington, D.C., and the plains of Pennsylvania.

"Remind Americans that freedom is worth dying for, so they should never take it for granted. And no matter what, we should finish the job we started, or I and every other marine, airman, sailor, and soldier who lost their limbs or lives in Iraq and Afghanistan will have done so in vain. Everybody on Earth deserves to be free—not just Americans and our coalition of friends. Our responsibility is not just to ourselves but also to the whole world. Most Iraqis I've met smile and wave and say, 'God Bless America.' I say it too: 'God Bless America!'"

I have become friends with Eddie and Robert, and we keep in touch. Every time I see a soldier, I always stop to shake his or her hand, think of Corporal James "Eddie" Wright, and say thanks!

Having seen the pure devotion and pride that this young man had in being a United States Marine and realizing his excitement to get his photograph taken in front of a World War II memorial as one of the "few and the proud," I must pay tribute before I conclude. Let us never forget the sacrifices so many have made day after day, year after year, dealing with the bad guys in war after war so you and I can be free to enjoy our freedoms.

Flying

We all have "bucket lists" that consist of exciting adventures we dream about achieving and accomplishing before we die. Because of my thirty-year involvement with the US military, my list has included flying every plane and helicopter in the US Air Force, Navy, Marines, and Army inventory. Depending on the aircraft, the sorties usually last for at least ninety minutes, wherein I have had the opportunity to fly them for thirty minutes.

So far I have flown the Black Hawk and Apache helicopters; the T-38, F-4, F-15, F-16, and F-18 fighter jets; the C-130, C-5, and C-17 transporters; the KC-10 and KC-135 tankers; the B-1, B-2, and B-52 bombers; and the U-2 spy plane, where for approximately three hours—at more than 70,000 feet—I saw the curvature of the earth, looked into the blackness of space, and pondered eternity and my place in it.

Anybody can learn to fly an airplane, but it takes a special individual to be a high-performance pilot. I have experienced this every time I have interacted with the US military. General Patton put it in perspective when he explained, "Wars may be fought with weapons, but they are won by men. It is the spirit of the men who follow and of the man who leads that gains the victory. If you are going to win any battle, you have to make the mind run the body. Never let the body tell the mind what to do."

I was an eyewitness to this at the end of 2000. I was invited to speak at the US Navy Commanders Conference at the Naval Museum in Pensacola, Florida. It was a wonderful experience, and I felt a deep connection with the audience of military brass. After my speech, the admirals congratulated me and said to let them know if there was anything they could ever do for me. I didn't even have to think about it. I quickly replied that I'd always dreamed of a backseat ride in an F-18 fighter jet. Without even blinking, US Marine pilot Colonel Eugene Frazier (call sign "Gator") said, "It's done. We can do that! Your training will be tough. We will cut you no slack. You're going to have to want it bad! Most VIPs have not made it through and did not get to fly. It's a gut check that is mind over matter—will over skill!"

On January 16, 2001, I went through five long, grueling hours of intense safety and survival training at the Naval Test Pilot School at Patuxent River, Maryland, in preparation for my flight the following morning. My first requirement was a complete physical examination by the flight surgeon.

Then it was off to "Aviation Physiology Water Survival Training." In eighty-five pounds of full combat gear, I had to swim fifty yards, two full lengths of an Olympic-size swimming pool (down and back), and then tread water for fifteen minutes. After a short rest out of the pool, with a blindfold mask covering my helmet, I then had to jump back in to find my way out of an underwater maze to simulate being trapped in the cockpit and keeping my wits about me to survive. Next, I sat through a lecture with diagrams and a test on "spatial disorientation." They strapped me into a souped-up bar stool with a seat belt, spun me around for five minutes, and had me get off and find my way to the door. (I felt like I was at a fraternity party in college!)

Next was "Egress Training," where I met a Rambo-looking guy, who, with a Southern accent, huge muscles, and a "yeehaw" look in his eye, asked, "Ya ever eject out of a jet before?" I sheepishly grunted the Scooby Doo "Hurh?" As he walked closer, I read his name-tag call sign: "Psycho." He immediately strapped me onto a tall torture-chamber-looking sled that rose to the ceiling at a forty-five-degree angle about fifty-five feet high. He smiled. "Keep your head up and back, knees straight, and elbows in, and on three, pull the yellow handle between your legs."

"What?"

"Three!"

I pulled and with three Gs of force squishing my body against itself, I shot up to the end of this ejection seat practice sled. We did it three times. Rambo then instructed me in the graceful art of flying and steering my parachute by hanging me from a ten-foot bar with straps that pinched me to where I didn't know if he had castrated me or was giving me a ninety-mile-an-hour enema! I was finally cut loose, concluding our wonderful time together by roll landing off a five-foot wall to simulate the hard landing.

Next on the training schedule was "Altitude Acclamation," where they took me to a room, fitted me with an oxygen mask, and simulated being at high altitude and losing air. I played a game of simply putting pegs into the correct round or square hole and thought I was doing it correctly. Come to find out on the video replay, I wasn't, and they documented at what level and point I began to lose my full faculties. They instructed me on what to do in case this lack of oxygen episode did occur. At day's end, I was required to take a classroom written exam on the contents and operation of every item in my survival vest, followed by a description of the cockpit gauges and "heads-up display," and how to hook up and release all the oxygen hoses, communication lines, safety belts, bells, and whistles.

Why do I itemize with such detail? Because I almost flunked the test! I nearly drowned three times! I was dizzy and exhausted, yet I continued on. Why? Of course it was to find Kelly McGillis in a washroom and get her to fall in love with me while I was flying Mach 2 with my hair on fire!

That night, I had a full five-course dinner with my host, Colonel Frazier, at the Officers Club. I asked him if there was anything special I should eat for breakfast, and he said, "Bananas."

"Why?" I asked. "Potassium? Will I cramp up?"

He said, "No, because bananas taste the same going in as they do coming out."

The next day, January 17, I flew with Commander Reuter—call sign "Roto"—on a ride to remember. There was no Cougar or Maverick or Iceman. I was putting my life in the hands of Roto Reuter! Turns out he was awesome and had more aircraft carrier takeoffs and landings than anyone else on base. The coolest thing was that he was a legitimate "Top Gunner"—one of the best of the best naval aviators. He even walked and smiled like Tom Cruise! Before we left the locker room to walk out on the tarmac, he taught me how to hold my helmet like a football in the crook of my elbow and how to walk and then stand like a real fighter pilot by the plane when we finally met the photographers for the "hero shots."

We took off in a straight-up, full, after-burner climb, and for the next ninety minutes, we did every *Top Gun* movie maneuver and more—loops, barrel rolls, yanks, and banks. We dived, climbed, and dived again with a vertical velocity of 10,000 feet per minute. We did ninety-degree turns at 600 mph, and for one special maneuver, climbed even higher to shoot straight down to pick up more speed (as if we weren't going fast enough as it was!). With my face now crammed up against the cockpit window, we climbed straight up to more than 55,000 feet, where you could actually begin to see the black sky and the curvature of the earth. Then we went upside down, flipped over to inside out, and flew in formation with a second aircraft we rendezvoused with. We executed attack bombing runs on a makeshift ship at the practice range in North Carolina, flew at 640 knots at only 500 feet off the ground, then went back to the thin air at 46,000 feet altitude where we broke the sound barrier going Mach 1.9 (around 1,200 mph—twice the speed of sound). We caught seven Gs in some of our turns (seven Gs meaning seven times my 235-pound body weight being smashed against my face, back, chest, kneecaps, and toes). I felt like somebody grabbed my bottom lip and pulled it up over my head. All this took place in a ninety-minute rock-and-roller-coaster ride every mentally irregular lunatic yearns for at Seven Flags over Hell Psycho Park. The highlight was my opportunity to fly the F-18 for thirty of the ninety minutes.

Before I share what I learned, let me confess to what everyone wonders. Colonel Frasier was absolutely right about the bananas, and yes, I egressed (ejected) all five dinner courses from the previous evening and even ejected some Hot Tamales I had eaten at a movie when I was nine! We were upside down so long that I am probably the only guy alive who has ever "thrown down"!

When we landed and I put my face back in the middle of my head, I asked Roto to point out some details about the plane. Commander Reuter explained that the F-18 Hornet is a state-of-the-art, high-tech, finely tuned and designed machine that costs $50 million to build. "Clark—call sign 'Hoss,'" he said (no one ever gets to choose their own call sign; I was very large for such a small cockpit and barely slid in), "the cockpit is crammed full of high-tech gauges, gadgets, switches, and screens. As you noticed, the control stick came out of the floor and was straddled between our knees. The stick only moved three inches forward, three inches left and right, and five inches backward. We needed to move the control stick only one inch in either one of those four directions, and it immediately changed the direction of the aircraft forty-five degrees." I then asked Roto how we flew this magnificent flying machine. His answer startled me. He flippantly said, "By feel."

Wow! We know the brain has two sides: the left cognitive/logical side and the right emotional/creative side. I find it interesting that we fly a high-tech, high-performance fighter jet with the touchy-feely right side of the brain. Shortly after this experience, I was given my first ride in an Air Force F-16 Falcon, wherein we caught 9.4 Gs and went Mach 1.1 while engaging in an air-to-air combat exercise where we chased another F-16 and then it chased us. Upon landing, I asked my pilot, Colonel Bill "Coutter" Couts, to explain how we flew this incredible F-16 with its patented "fly-by-wire" control grip that only moved one-eighth to three-eighths of an inch. He answered, "Hot Lips" (yes, that is my Air Force call sign!), "when you climbed up the ladder to slide into the cockpit, did you strap into the F-16, or did you strap the F-16 on to you?"

Hmmm. Life 101? Motivation 101? The only thing we are not in charge of is whether or not we are in charge. High-performance leadership, management, coaching, teaching, parenting, and living is about Figuring It Out, Feeling It, and Flying!

Humanitarian Warriors

So much of what our soldiers do reflects a willingness to sacrifice for the sake of our ideals without any expectation of a return. Although media coverage focuses mainly on battle carnage, the truth is that our troops are not just fighting enemies; they are engaging in diplomatic service and the humanitarian side of freedom and liberation from tyranny. They are going beyond commitment and giving of themselves in accordance with their highest beliefs and principles.

According to CNN, between 2003 and 2008, U.S. and Coalition forces in Iraq built more than 4,000 schools stocked with 8 million books and built more than 250 hospitals with state-of-the-art equipment. As a result, 98 percent of Iraq's children are getting to go to school for the first time and have now been vaccinated for diseases, including polio and tuberculosis. Furthermore, 25 percent of Iraq's Parliament is now made up of women—the highest percentage in any Arab country—more than 33,000 new businesses have started up, and more than 5 million Iraqis use mobile phones.

With their numbers shrinking, our men and women in uniform created and equipped a new Iraqi Air Force, disarmed the regional militias, trained and equipped well over 19,000 elite Iraqi special forces soldiers, trained more than 18,000 border patrol officers who enforce the Syrian and Iranian borders, and have recruited and trained thousands of provincial and local police officers to keep the neighborhood peace.

Our brave soldiers always give something more—sometimes they give it all. For this reason, I hope you will join me in stepping up our support for our troops.

Homecoming

I was traveling to Chicago on business. As I settled into my seat on the plane, a marine sergeant was invited to sit in the first-class seat across from me. The sergeant was sitting tall and proud in his uniform and was holding a folded American flag. I turned to the marine and inquired if he was heading home or heading out.

"Neither," he answered, "I'm escorting a soldier home."

"Going to pick him up?" I asked.

"No," the marine answered. "He is with me right now. He was killed in Iraq. I'm taking him home to his family and presenting this flag to his mother."

The realization of what the marine had been asked to do hit me like a punch to the gut. It was an honor for this marine to do this. He told me that although he did not know the fallen soldier, he had been the one who had delivered the sad news of his death to the family and felt as if he knew them after the many conversations they had shared in the last few days. I leaned across to him, extended my hand, and said, "Thank you. Thank you for doing what you do so that my family and I can enjoy peace of mind and be free, with security and safety, to do what we want to do."

Upon landing in Chicago, the pilot stopped short of the gate and made the following announcement over the intercom. "Ladies and Gentlemen, we have had the honor of having Sergeant Seeley of the United States Marine Corps join us on this flight. He is escorting a fallen comrade who was killed in action back home to his family. I ask that you remain in your seats when we open the forward door to allow Sergeant Seeley to deplane and receive his fellow soldier. We will then turn off the seat belt sign." Without a sound, all went as requested. As I watched out my window, I saw the sergeant saluting the casket as it was brought off the plane.

There wasn't a dry eye on the aircraft as everyone who witnessed this sacred and intimate display of duty, honor, love of country, and reverent devotion to service above self felt proud to be Americans.

This sacred experience continued to change my attitude and behavior toward our brave servicemen and women forever. It has changed the way I think about the flag and all that it stands for, which, consequently, has also changed the way I say the Pledge of Allegiance. Let us never forget that "it is the soldier, not the poet, who gave us freedom of speech. It is the soldier, not the reporter, who gave us freedom of the press. It is the soldier, not the campus organizer, who gave us freedom to demonstrate. And it is the soldier who salutes the flag, who serves under the flag, whose coffin is draped by the flag, who has given the insensitive fanatics the freedom to burn the flag."

Killer Chick

Let me tell you about a smart, talented, tenacious, beautiful, petite, blond, compassionate yet intense, courageous friend of mine who flies one of the coolest jets in the world. Meet A-10 fighter pilot and war hero, Mrs. Kim Campbell.

The A-10 is an impressive airplane designed to get down low and provide close air support (CAS) for the soldiers on the ground. This meant building the aircraft around a nineteen-foot-long 30mm Gatling gun and designing the cockpit as a titanium bathtub to provide extra protection for the pilot. It's a tough plane built to take some hits while performing its mission. Capt. Campbell became an eyewitness to this fact and in her own words shares her experience of juggling and harmony:

> On a CAS mission I flew on April 7 over downtown Baghdad, we were originally tasked to target some Iraqi tanks and vehicles in the city that were acting as a command post and to take out the prominent North Baghdad Bridge. But en route to the target area, we received a call from the ground forward air controller saying they were taking fire and needed immediate assistance. They were on the west side of the Tigris River, and units of the Iraqi Republican Guard were on the east side firing rocket-propelled grenades into our guys.
>
> We stayed above the weather as long as possible and then once over the target area, descended through the clouds to positively identify both the friendly troops and the enemy location. It was definitely a high-threat situation, and we immediately unloaded our guns and high-explosive rockets down on the enemy.
>
> After my last rocket pass, I was maneuvering off target when I felt and heard a large explosion at the back of my jet. I knew immediately that I had been hit by enemy fire. My jet rolled violently left and pointed nose first at the city below, not

251

responding to my control inputs. Luckily, my training kicked in and I was able to react very quickly. I checked the hydraulic gauges and both read zero. This meant no steering and, if I was able to land, no brakes. My only option at this point was to put the jet into "manual reversion" as the backup system. Manual reversion is a system of cranks and cables that allow the pilot to fly the aircraft under mechanical control, similar to driving an automobile that has just lost its power steering. It was my last chance to try and recover the aircraft, or I would be riding a parachute down into central Baghdad where surely I would be captured, most likely raped, dragged through the streets by the insurgents, beheaded, and hung from a bridge to be seen by my family and friends on CNN.

Apparently this grim reality motivated me, because after some serious teeth-gritting, muscle-straining yanks and energy-draining pulls, I got my magnificent A-10 to start climbing out and away. We started maneuvering south when AAA [anti-aircraft artillery] ground fire started coming up from everywhere. I couldn't do much to move the jet around, so I was hoping that the theory of "big sky, little bullet" would work in my favor.

Due to the design of the A-10, I couldn't see the damage to my jet, even with the use of my cockpit mirrors. However, my flight lead did an initial battle damage check and told me that I had a lot of holes in the fuselage and tail section on the right side, as well as a football-size hole on the right horizontal stabilizer. He also said the right engine had caught fire but somehow had extinguished itself. Suddenly I had to make a decision. Do I stay with the jet and try to land it back at the base or get to friendly territory and eject?

As pilots, we don't train very often in manual reversion, and in the checklist, it says to attempt a manual reversion landing only under ideal conditions. I knew that A-10 manual reversion landings had been attempted three times during Desert Storm, but not all had been successful. One pilot was killed when his jet crashed over the runway threshold. Another aircraft was severely damaged after touching down, only to find out that [the pilot] had no brakes. However, there was a glimmer of hope in that the third manual reversion landing was in an aircraft with similar damage to mine, and it had been successful. The odds weren't great, but every situation is different, and I was confident that I was going to land my jet safely.

The flight back to Kuwait was probably one of the longest hours of my life. I didn't know exactly what was going to happen when I configured the aircraft and attempted to land. As we crossed into friendly territory, I once again descended through the clouds to start the controllability check. As I slowed the aircraft, it immediately became much harder to hold steady and started descending uncontrollably toward the ground. I thought I might once again have to eject, but I completed the procedure for emergency gear extension and the landing gear came down with three green lights telling me they were locked.

The only thing left was to find the runway through the standard haze associated with the continual dust storms in Kuwait. I contacted the tower to let him know I was on my way in. The crash recovery team was waiting for me and the rescue helicopters were on alert in case I had to eject. I was hoping that I wouldn't need either, but it was good to know they were there. As I crossed the landing threshold, the aircraft started a quick roll to the left that, luckily, I was able to counteract with the flight controls and continue with my landing. When all three wheels hit the ground, it was an amazing feeling of relief, but I still had to get the jet stopped. I accomplished the emergency procedure for alternate braking and once again, the jet worked as advertised. And because I was so focused on what was possible to get, it turned out that my landing was one of the best ones I had ever done!

When I finally got the jet stopped and climbed out of the cockpit, the wing commander and recovery crews immediately greeted me, as we all were anxious to see the battle damage. There were more than a hundred bullet holes in the tail, and shrapnel had taken out the right horizontal stabilizer, the primary flight control, and the right rudder cable. The weapons experts believe that a surface-to-air missile hit the back of the jet, which sheared the left and right hydraulic lines in two different locations, sending shrapnel through the right side of the aircraft. The backside of the jet was charred from the engine fire and covered with hydraulic fluid.

What I didn't know as I was making my way back to base was that a description of my battle damage had already made its way to the other pilots, our maintainers, and base personnel. On my approach, I could see them standing along the runway watching, praying, and waving to welcome me home. More well-wishers were assembled at the A-10 ramp. Of course, it was a huge relief to be back on the ground, but the best part was hearing the guys in my squadron on the radio as I rolled down the runway. Several had been standing by in their jets waiting to launch until they saw me safely return. I will never forget their cheers and the encouraging, complimentary words that I heard that day.

On April 8, the day after this life-and-death situation, we were sitting in our alert shack when we got the call that an A-10 pilot had been shot down near Baghdad. We scrambled to our jets and made an immediate takeoff. After about thirty minutes of flight time, we received a call that we could return to base. The pilot had been picked up by some of our forces on the ground and he was in good hands with American forces.

I never really had time to think about the fact that I was going back to Baghdad where just the day before I had narrowly escaped being shot down. In my mind, the only thing that I could think about was that I had a job to do. There was a pilot on the ground and he needed our help. I knew that the Search and Rescue crews were there for me the day before, and I was going to do the same for this pilot. I am so proud to be an attack pilot in the United States Air Force, and I willingly fly into harm's way so people can be free on the ground. I couldn't ask for a better job!

When TV journalist Diane Sawyer was in Iraq on a special assignment and heard this story about Kim Campbell, Ms. Sawyer tracked her down for an interview as she returned from a mission. Seeing "KC" painted on the side of her new jet, Ms. Sawyer asked Kim what it stood for. With a mischievous grin, Kim replied, "Killer Chick." Knowing what you now know, there is no reason for any of us to believe otherwise!

Miracle Mission

I proudly serve as a member of the International Board of Governors of Operation Smile, a humanitarian organization whose plastic surgeons and critical care pediatric nurses volunteer their time to perform cleft lip and palate surgeries on underprivileged, needy children throughout the world. As of 2011, our teams have operated on more than 150,000 children in fifty-five developing countries, and have conducted more than one hundred missions per year worldwide. In 2005, my daughter and I accompanied our Operation Smile medical staff to Vietnam, where in a four-and-a-half-day period, our team performed 162 surgeries, transforming these precious children from hard-to-look-at, ridiculed, ostracized ciphers into beautiful children who finally feel life is worth living.

My favorite Operation Smile experience happened in Iraq, where our team planned to operate on 110 Iraqi children who had severe facial deformities, including twenty-nine under the age of two. A mission was organized to transport the children with their parents, medical volunteers, and nine Iraqi doctors (210 people total) across the desert in several buses on a twenty-four-hour ride to Amman, Jordan. Halfway there, terrorist insurgents boarded the buses, screaming, pointing guns and knives, and demanding that any of the rival religious faction be identified and dragged off the buses to be executed. No one responded. Miraculously, thirty minutes later, the terrorists got off the buses without hurting anyone and disappeared into the night. The frightened Iraqi families and medical volunteers continued to Amman, and within days, the 110 surgeries had been successfully completed.

All 210 people on this mission were terrified at the idea of making the long bus ride home. Even the bus drivers refused to go. I received a phone call from my dear friend Michael Nebeker, whose sister Susan was on this mission and had reported the details to him over the phone. Then the co-founders of Operation Smile, Dr. Bill Magee and his wife Kathy, called to see if I could use my relationship with the US Air Force to help. I had just spoken at the World Command Chiefs Conference for my friend and hero Gerald Murray, Command Chief Master Sergeant of the Air Force, so I phoned him right after hanging up with Dr. Magee. Knowing how important it is for the United States to win hearts and minds with "soft power," Murray said he could get this thing done if we generated a "sponsor letter" from a senator or congressman.

Senator John Warner (R-Virginia) and Congressman Trent Franks (D-Arizona), with the incredible support from my dear friend Senator Orrin Hatch (R-Utah), composed the letter and then hand-delivered it to Defense Secretary Rumsfeld. Chief Murray then counseled with Air Force chief of staff General T. Michael Moseley, and within twenty-four hours, two C-17 transport jets were sent from Baghdad to Amman to rescue these 210 people. When they landed safely at the Baghdad International Airport, the families and medical volunteers walked down the stairs with their now beautiful babies and brand-new smiles. They knelt down in thanksgiving to kiss the ground of their homeland, and then stood to cheer and thank the military men and women who had loved them and unselfishly served them that day.

Clearly, Dr. Bill and Kathy Magee are international angels of love, hope, mercy, and medical miracles. Operation Smile creates medical diplomacy everywhere it goes and epitomizes what it means to be an international citizen of the world. Learn how to get involved at www.operationsmile.org, and discover how both the giver and the receiver of covenant service are transformed from successful to significant.

Lyrical Poetry

Special Man

A little boy wants to be like his dad
So he watches us night and day.
He mimics our moves and weighs our words
He steps in our steps all the way.
He's sculpting a life we're the model for
He'll follow us happy or sad,
And his future depends on example set
'Cause the little boy wants to be just like his dad.
A special man talks by example,
Takes the time to play and hug his lad,
A special man walks by example,
The very best friend a growing boy ever had.
Any male can be a father,
But it takes a special man to be a dad.
He needs a hero to emulate,
He breathes "I believe in you."
Would we have him see everything we see
And have him do everything that we do?
When we see the reverence that sparkles and shines
In the worshipping eyes of our lad,
Will we be at peace if his dreams come true
And he grows up to be just like his dad?

258

Real Man

I need a man
Who knows happily ever after
Is a day-at-a-time proposition,
A man who knows makin' love
Is not a three-minute composition;
It's a slow dance, full of romance,
A walk on the beach in the sand,
It's having a whole conversation, just by holding my hand.
He would stir deep desire that sets me on fire
To be with him all that I can.
No, no, I won't settle for anything less than a real man.
A real man's strong in stature,
Firm in faith and kisses slow.
He sometimes cries, and when we hug
He's the last one to let go.
Worshipping the ground I walk on, he's my biggest fan,
There's nothin' like being loved by a Real Man!
I need a man
Who knows honoring me and my dreams
Is a macho disposition,
A man who knows "I love you"
Is a more-than-words condition.
It's roses for no reason, secret love notes in my drawer,
It's making me his equal, yet he always gets my door.

He would never raise his hand to me, believes in who I am,
Yeah, I can be more than I thought I could be, with a Real Man.
You talk to me through touch,
I'm swept away in every clutch,
We're lovers but we're best friends too,
I like me best when I'm with you . . .

U-2 Eternity

On October 22 and 23, 2010, I had a pinnacle adventure in a "high flight" aboard a U-2 reconnaissance spy plane. After a flight surgeon gave me a comprehensive examination at the base clinic, the fitting and donning of my pressurized astronaut space suit was complete, and I had finished a half day of ejection seat and cardio training—and physiological and pressurization tests in the altitude chamber—I was ready for my flight.

The next morning at 6:00 AM, we repeated most of the ordeal, boarded the aircraft with my pilot Gino, and, in a high-performance takeoff where the thick clouds miraculously opened in the nick of time to create a small window of blue sky through which we could climb toward heaven, we accelerated straight up to soar on the edge of the universe. At the breathtaking, classified altitude of more than 70,000 feet, and with tears in my eyes that kept fogging up my helmet visor, I saw the curvature of the earth, witnessed the majesty and endless blackness of space, and, at fifteen miles above the earth's surface, literally gazed into eternity. (The fifteen-minute documentary is on YouTube at Dan Clark U2 Spy Plane.)

Part of the spiritual experience for me was realizing that for those few hours, Gino and I were higher than any other human beings on planet Earth, with the exception of the few astronauts and cosmonauts living in the space station. It hit me hard that the only things we can take with us when we die are what I had with me in the aircraft: my character, my convictions, and my education; and that what we leave behind is what I left on the ground: my reputation and a legacy that included taking the time to make a difference in the lives of my family, friends, and fellow citizens. What we do for ourselves dies with us. What we do for others and the world remains and is immortal. I now know that having success is no longer a substitute for being significant. Now is the time to minimize our hope for success and maximize the effort required to become significant by focusing not on what's impressive but on what's important. This three-and-a-half-hour flight inspired the following poem:

U-2 Eternity

Today I woke, prepared myself both physically and mentally,
And breathed only the purest thoughts to free myself
from every negativity, then suited up and walked to board
a secret craft to soar beyond the bonds of life's ordinary gravity.
Up, straight up I shot, and danced with clouds until I climbed
above them in high flight to see as far as I could see.
I saw the curvature of Earth, and on the edge of space,
if we're alone, a waste of space it is for all humanity.
And in the blackness of our universe, suspended on the wind above
where eagles fly, with grace I hovered, sensing that the best is yet to be.
Where in the sounds of silence realized what we take with us
in death is what I had with me: education, character, and
a "made-a-difference" legacy. Then, with tear-filled eyes,
surreal in a tranquil blue serenity, my heart stood still in breathtaking humility.
As I, in awe, felt His almighty presence while I gazed into eternity.

Unstoppable

One of the true heroes in my life is the collegiate wrestling champion Anthony Robles. In 2011, Anthony won the National NCAA Wrestling Championship—with only one leg! I was privileged to be asked to write his acceptance speech as he proudly received the Jimmy Valvano ESPY Award for Courage on national television July 14, 2011. With the world watching, Robles humbly spoke:

"At the beginning of my wrestling career, I lost most of my matches, and people said, 'It's okay. I'm proud of you for trying.' This ticked me off so bad! Losing is not okay! What they were really saying was that I was a handicapped kid and should be grateful that I could even participate.

"My dear mother had me when she was sixteen-years-old. It was the summer before her senior year in high school. My birth dad immediately bailed. I was born with one leg, and my mom could have walked away and given me up for adoption. She didn't. While kids at school made fun of me, she taught me to never let what I cannot do interfere with what I can do.

"She could have protected me from pain and failure, but she knew it would develop my character and make me strong. So she even let me play football. And even when my mom got sick at the beginning of my sophomore year in college, and my stepdad walked out on our family and we lost our home, and I wanted to quit wrestling to get a job and help pay the bills, still my mom refused to let any of us give up!"

Robles concluded with a poem I wrote that uses his incredible personal story to convey the intensely personal nature of winning:

Unstoppable

Every soul who comes to earth
With a leg or two at birth
Must wrestle his opponents knowing
It's not what is, it's what can be, that measures worth.
Make it hard, just make it possible,
And through pain, I'll not complain,
My spirit is unconquerable.
Fearless I will face each foe,
For I know I am capable,
Making winning personal
I don't care what's probable,
Through blood, sweat, and tears,
I am Unstoppable!

© Dan Clark 2011

Quiet Heroes

The world is full of quiet heroes who never seek the praise,
They're always back off in the shadows,
They let us have the limelight days.
For this you're the one that I look up to,
Because of you I'm free,
You set an example I could follow,
You helped me see my destiny.
So even though my thanks don't show,
Unnoticed you will never go,
I need to say I love you so,
You're my hero.
I've had my share of broken dreams,
But you said I could win.
You gave me the chance I always needed to start my dreams again.
You took the time to teach and tutor and show me rules to rise,
You changed my fears to glory tears,
You're an angel in disguise.
I wouldn't be where I am today, I've won my share of times,
Unless you coached me through the maze and pushed me on the hardest climbs.
It's just your style, the extra mile, no glory must be tough,
You let me have the accolades,
A smile, you said, was just enough.

Parable of the Eagle

The bald eagle is the most magnificent bird—the ultimate symbol of freedom, strength, loyalty, honor, majesty, and grace. When our Founding Fathers were selecting a national symbol, John Adams pushed for the dove as the symbol of peace. Benjamin Franklin wanted the turkey for its cunning. Thank God they agreed on Thomas Jefferson's suggestion of the mighty eagle—it represents:

Freedom—Soaring upwards of hundreds of feet in the sky, its eyesight is nine times greater than that of any human. When hunting, it folds back its wings to dive straight down at speeds of 100 miles an hour.

Strength—The female weighs between twelve and fourteen pounds with a wingspan of six feet and is larger than the nine-pound male. Its talons have the gripping strength of 204 times that of a very strong, muscle-bound man. The eagle builds the largest nests of any bird; some nests weigh 2,000 pounds.

Loyalty—Eagles mate for life and return to the same nest year after year to hatch their young.

Honor—The parents teach their offspring everything they know about flying, hunting, building a nest, selecting the right nesting site, and even choosing the perfect lifelong mate. Only then do the adults send the baby birds out into the world to soar on their own.

Majesty and Grace—Eagles have no natural enemies, are respected by man and beast, go where they want to go, and soar in the clouds above the highest cliffs for hours at a time without any rest.

If only we could fully comprehend the "Parable of the Eagle."

A farmer in Wyoming was walking through the forest and found a newborn eagle that had fallen from its nest. He took it home, nursed it back to full strength, and put it in the chicken coop to raise it. A few years later, a Native American naturalist stopped by the farmer's house and noticed the full-grown bird. "What is that eagle doing in the chicken coop? It isn't right that an eagle should be kept with chickens." The Native American picked up the bird and said, "Thou hast the heart of an eagle. Thou dost belong to the sky and not to the earth. Stretch forth thy wings and fly."

The bird looked around outside its comfort zone, but quickly saw the chickens and dropped to the ground. "See, I told you it was a chicken," the farmer bragged. "I have trained it as a chicken, and it thinks and pecks and walks like a chicken."

The naturalist exclaimed, "No, no, it is a mighty eagle." He took the bird and stood on top of the farmer's shed. "Stretch forth thy wings and fly," he said. But once again, the eagle saw its chicken friends below and jumped down to peck with them.

Early the next morning, the naturalist revisited the farm and took the bird from the chicken coop to the base of a great mountain. In classic Native American tradition, he held the bird high over his head and bellowed loud enough for his voice to echo and bounce off the cliff walls. "Thou art an eagle. Thou hast the heart of an eagle. Thou dost belong to the wind and the sky and not unto the earth. Stretch forth thy wings and fly."

The eagle looked down uncomfortably, but the naturalist forced it to look directly into the sun. A moment passed and then, with a screech, it stretched forth its wings and flew.

Sometimes we fail to dream mighty dreams and fail to soar to the heights that the eagle in each of us can attain because we have our eyes down with the chickens. We are pecking and grabbing about because we lack self-confidence and self-esteem. And so we minimize our own worth. We are groping because we're missing the link that connects us from where we are to where we want to be. Don't you think it is now time to start seeing yourself as you really are, an eagle soaring above the average, negative crowd? You were born to succeed. Stretch forth *your* wings and fly!

Clark's Credo

- I'm smart, talented, and I never say never.
- I'm wanted, important, lovable, capable, and I can succeed.
- I have pride, class, flexibility, grace, discipline, and balance.
- I'm a good athlete, I love music, and I get good grades in school.
- I never say "I can't"—I always say "I can, I will."
- If I fall down or fail, I just get back up and try again.
- If I spill or make a mistake, I learn why, clean it up, and say "no big deal."
- I treat others as I want to be treated.
- I always tell the truth and play by the rules.
- I dream mighty dreams. If I don't dream, how can I make a dream come true?
- I love God and will do the right thing simply because it's the right thing to do!
- Therefore, I leave no regrets by always leaving my family, friends, job, neighborhood, country, and world in better shape than I found them. I'm somebody very special. No one can ever take my place. Whenever I leave, everybody says, "I like me best when I'm with you. I want to see you again.